THE LIVING ROOM SERIES

NO OTHER GODS

confronting our
modern-day idols

kelly minter

© 2007, LifeWay Press®
Second Printing July 2008

ISBN 978-1-4158-5256-9
Item number 005035500

This book is the text for course CG-1307 in the subject area Bible Studies in the Christian Growth Study Plan.

Dewey Decimal Classification: 231.7
Subject Heading: BIBLE--STUDY \ GOD \ CHRISTIAN LIFE

Unless otherwise noted, Scripture quotations are from the Holy Bible, New International Version, copyright © 1973, 1978, 1984 by International Bible Society.

Scripture quotations marked HCSB® are taken from the Holman Christian Standard Bible®, copyright © 1999, 2000, 2001, 2002 by Holman Bible Publishers. Used by permission.

Scripture quotations marked KJV are from the King James Version of the Bible.

To order additional copies of this resource, write LifeWay Church Resources Customer Service; One LifeWay Plaza; Nashville, TN 37234-0113; FAX order to (615) 251-5933; call toll-free 1-800-458-2772; e-mail *orderentry@lifeway.com;* order online at *www.lifeway.com;* or visit the LifeWay Christian Store serving you.

Printed in the United States of America

Leadership and Adult Publishing
LifeWay Church Resources
One LifeWay Plaza
Nashville, TN 37234-0175

TABLE OF CONTENTS

NO OTHER GODS: CONFRONTING OUR MODERN-DAY IDOLS

SESSION 1 PERSONAL PHARAOHS 8
BLACK BEANS AND RICE & BUTTERFINGER CAKE . . . 28

SESSION 2 WHY IDOLS? 30
BECKER'S PASTA & CAPRESE SALAD 52

SESSION 3 LIES 54
CARRIE'S CHICKEN SCALLOPINI 75

SESSION 4 THE PROBLEM WITH IDOLS 76
EASY BEEF POT ROAST & PUMPKIN MUFFINS 96

SESSION 5 GOOD GOODBYES 98
SICILIAN PIZZA CRUST 119

SESSION 6 GOD OF GODS 120
GRANDMA'S MAC AND CHEESE & TOSSED SALAD . . . 140

SESSION 7 THE ROAD AHEAD 142
CHICKEN CUTLETS WITH MOM'S SAUCE 160

SESSION 8 MAKING ROOM 162
LAURI'S SECRET RECIPE CHILI 183

LEADER GUIDE 184

MEET THE AUTHOR
KELLY MINTER

Kelly Minter keeps an exciting schedule as an author, songwriter, worship leader, speaker, and musician—a list that's likely to keep growing as she continues to discover new talents. Kelly got her start as a recording artist. Her 2001 major-label debut, *Good Day,* garnered critical acclaim, and its follow-up, 2003's *Wrestling the Angels,* built on that solid foundation and had a number one hit, "This is My Offering." In 2005, however, Kelly sensed God urging her to stop striving and lay everything down. She let go of her management and label ties to pursue God's new path for her. Since then, she has led worship at a church nearly every weekend.

Kelly is releasing a worship record with Kingsway and appearing on a live worship DVD entitled *Worship at the Abbey.* The multi-artist project was recorded at England's famed Abbey Road.

Kelly lives in Nashville, Tennessee, when she isn't on the road leading worship and speaking at conferences such as LifeWay's After Eve and Daybreak. She also writes extensively; she is the author of *Water Into Wine: Hope for the Miraculous In the Struggle of the Mundane* (2004, Waterbrook Press) as well as several forthcoming projects. As a songwriter, she has had her music recorded by Point of Grace, Joy Williams, Sonicflood, Sandi Patty, and Margaret Becker.

For information on Kelly's schedule and resources, see *www.kellyminter.com.*

Jessica Weaver wrote the leader guide. She is an editor at LifeWay. A graduate of the University of Richmond, Jessica majored in English and minored in Chinese. She resides in Nashville, Tennessee, with her husband Adam and their cocker spaniel, Chester. She enjoys singing in the choir and teaching children at Forest Hills Baptist Church, where she and Adam are active members.

INTRODUCTION

LET ME FIRST START OFF BY SAYING THAT I'M SO GLAD YOU'RE HERE ... ACTUALLY, THAT MIGHT BE A BIT PRESUMPTUOUS ON MY PART. LET ME BACK UP A MOMENT. MAYBE YOU'RE NOT "HERE" YET. MAYBE YOU'RE STILL BROWSING, CHECKING OUT THE COVER, THE TOPIC, THE INTRO. PERHAPS YOU'RE NOT QUITE SOLD. NOT TOTALLY CONVINCED YOU WANT TO SPEND THE NEXT EIGHT WEEKS DELVING INTO THE MODERN-DAY IDOLS IN YOUR LIFE WITH A GROUP OF FRIENDS. YOU MAY BE THINKING ... THAT'S NOT NEARLY AS MUCH FUN AS IT SOUNDS. IN WHICH CASE, YOU ARE PROBABLY RIGHT, THOUGH I WILL TELL YOU THAT THE PROCESS IS FAR MORE REWARDING THAN IT IS "UN-FUN."

A few years ago I was feeling stuck. Stuck with God, people, career, living space, finances, convictions. I constantly cried out to God, "Please deliver me." My prayers were simple, often alternating between the profoundly passionate and the nearly numb. Where was God? Who was He? What was my life supposed to look like? Were true relationships possible? And on and on ... (All this from someone who loved and grew up with God, the Bible, and His church.)

I was not ready for the simplicity of God's remedy; He wanted to be God in my life.

Though somewhat unaware, I had been depending on false gods that were at the bottom of much of my pain. They were taking up room in my heart—room God desired to occupy. Through this process I became desperate to discover who the true God was in all of His glory so as not return to the lesser and baser things. These idols could only offer temporary relief—promising what they could never deliver. How relieved I've been to find that through the dismantling, God has planted, built, restored, and redeemed. He has done nothing short of the miraculous.

The whole idea of false gods was a quick word, though anything but a quick fix. It marked the beginning of a life-changing process for me. A journey that required some tearing down of the things that were taking the place of God in my life. Not for the sake of destruction, however, but for the promise of the new, the strong, and the life-giving.

If you are still with me, still considering if you want to engage with your life this intimately, wondering if it is worth the journey, let me throw out one more thing ... you can walk this road in a living room. With conversation. With friends. With food. With music. With prayer. No pretenses. No legalism.

Enhancing the experience is also the addition of a Web site complete with blogs, podcasts, book and music recommendations, picture sharing, an online community, forums, and more. Check out *www.lifeway.com/livingroomseries* for the full experience.

Are you with me? Are you committing? (So sorry to use the "c" word here.) Would it at all help if I further persuaded you by introducing four more friends who will be somewhat along for the ride? Meet Carrie, Lauri, Anadara, and Alli. You'll get to know them better in the weeks ahead and on the web, but they're crazy, fun, smart, deep, thinking women. One is about to have a baby, one's been in a movie, and two are touring artists. They love God, and dare I say they are actually somewhat normal? You must be intrigued.

All else aside, it would be one of my greatest honors to walk with you through one of the most profound roads I've ever taken with the Lord. Anything He prompts us to release will only be restored to us in overflowing measures. (Whoever loses his life will gain it.) Through all the pain, loneliness, and difficulty, I have found God to be deeply satisfying, good, and faithful despite my wandering heart. It is my desperate hope you will find Him the same.

If any of this is resonating with you, I hope you will consider this eight-week holistic approach to looking into Scripture and discovering God in the midst of likeminded, yet vastly unique, individuals who might be on a similar journey. Not to mention the food. Carrie, Lauri, Anadara, Alli, and I are saying no to bad casseroles, powdered lemonade, and frozen lasagna. Recipes we've used for our own dinners are scattered throughout the book and Web site, along with favorite quotes, reading recommendations, and play lists. So light a candle, bring your iPod, and don't burn your pine nuts (happens all the time to me). A depth of supernatural revelation hovers in a study that will require your heart and mind, while in a setting that will feed your body and soul. Come sit.

Kelly

PERSONAL PHARAOHS
DEFINING OUR TERMS

IT ALL STARTED LAST WEDNESDAY NIGHT AT MY HOUSE.

JULY 29TH TO BE EXACT. FOUR GIRLS—LAURI, ALLI, ANADARA, AND CARRIE—CAME OVER FOR DINNER. SOME WERE MEETING FOR THE FIRST TIME; SOME HAD KNOWN EACH OTHER FOR A WHILE. ALL ARE MARRIED, EXCEPT ME. I AM THE LONE SINGLE IN THE BUNCH.

I thought it would be interesting to see what would happen if we committed to getting together once a week for a two-month Bible study I was writing on a topic I wasn't sure of yet. I know. It sounds riveting. Which is why I had to offer dinner as part of the package. Which is also why I had to start learning how to cook, because despite my wonderful upbringing in the church, I just didn't think I could stand one more potluck or frozen lasagna. I was longing for a home with a couch, cookies, and anything warmer than fluorescent lighting. I wanted to talk about the deeper issues of life in a setting where we felt comfortable. Mostly, I was committed to avoiding pat Christian answers, hopefully diving past the rhetoric and into the life-changing revelation of Scripture.

So I invited everyone over and served a black bean and brown rice recipe I picked up from a friend in New York. She grew up working in her father's restaurant, not to mention she's fully Italian, so culinary magic lives up her sleeve. Once while I was visiting she made me the black bean and brown rice dinner, and it was so delectably overwhelming that it's all I can remember about the night. So I asked my friend for the recipe, and of course, she said the three words that terrify me most, the words that clinch imminent failure: "It's soooo easy." I would rather someone tell me how incredibly daunting a task is, so if the whole thing ends up as charcoal I won't feel so bad. And if I end up wildly succeeding I will have something to prop up my self-esteem at least until the morning.

Once I got over how "easy" all this was going to be, she further mentioned that she really didn't have a recipe, and I might just have to feel my way through it: A little of this, a little of that, set the oven on three-something-or-other until it looks about done. So I am a non-cook now using a non-recipe for one of my first ever dinner parties. I'm almost sad to say that it turned out great and the evening was seamless—it just doesn't make for nearly as interesting of a story. The recipe's at the end of the chapter and to further assist you I want to emphatically state that this is a very tricky meal to make.

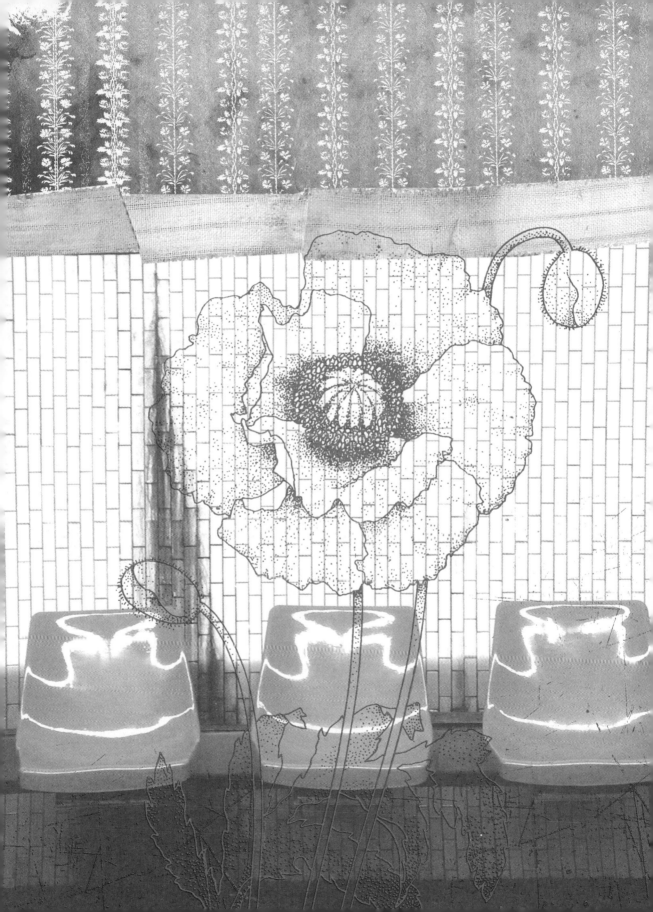

After our black bean dinner we moved from the kitchen to my living room, about a 27-inch journey, as I live in a space almost equivalent to a walk-in closet. We made ourselves comfortable and naturally fell into a conversation about life-purpose, body image, media influence, perfectionism, finding identity in marriage and singleness, our desire to live uniquely, measuring up, battling loneliness, wanting something "more" in life. Okay, so it wasn't light. This was our first time together so it was more of a focus group for me to gather information hoping to find a topic of study that might apply.

The conversation was something like popcorn popping, sporadic yet steady. I think it was Anadara, a talented singer/songwriter, who piped up seemingly out of nowhere, "I refuse to send out Christmas cards this year." It was July. We were confused. "Anadara, can you clarify a bit?"

"I'm just tired of the same old, same old. Sending out Christmas cards with a picture of my husband and me feels like the epitome of the expected. I feel stuck in a rut of nominal routines. I want to do something different." Her reluctance to produce mass copies of herself and her smiling husband stamped with *peace on earth* suddenly made perfect sense.

Alli, the youngest in our group, with wisdom well beyond her years, relayed sympathizing thoughts, "I guess I feel like there's a mold we're 'supposed' to fit and none of us are making the cut. We don't feel good enough. We feel bad, guilty. Yet we don't want to do the same thing as everyone else and lose ourselves in the process."

Our in-house makeup artist and actress, Lauri, chimed in with a personal story: "I had an evaluation at work the other day and all I could think about was the one negative thing mentioned. I couldn't even remember all the positive statements my boss had made about me. I could only chew on the small area that was lacking. I totally felt like a failure. I don't know why I'm so debilitated by criticism." Carrie, our smart-as-a-whip businesswoman, noted, "I think we put an increased expectation for our accomplishments on ourselves. We let what people think of us affect us."

I added to Carrie's statement, "I think so many perceived standards out there bellow from the media and culture, and even the church, about what we are to do, weigh, wear, look like, act like. The constant bombardment of expectations is now so commonplace I'm not sure we're even aware of the heavy burdens that come with trying to fulfill them." We touched on these and many more issues. Nothing was out of bounds as we discussed our struggles and questions within a Christian framework.

As expected in a group of church-exposed girls, we had the usual solutions and the anticipated answers: Freedom in Christ, Identity in Christ, Knowing Christ. I think we unanimously identified all three as foundational to dealing with any of the issues. But I'm not sure we know what these things actually look like. All of us were quick to admit that our understanding and implementation of identity and freedom in Christ were mostly confused and rarely experienced.

After the girls left I got into bed and flipped on the TV. I started with a popular sitcom. After five minutes of raunchy innuendo, I then breezed through a terribly explicit sexual something-or-other that I fortunately didn't have time to make out before landing on a news channel. It was displaying slow motion reruns of people falling from a stadium ledge that had crumbled beneath them. Perhaps the home improvement networks would offer something void of sex and tragedy. So I tuned in to the story of a man who had finally achieved his lifelong dream of having a stainless steel espresso maker built into his wall, because life simply wasn't full enough unless he could froth his coffee in the morning without having to plug in a freestanding machine. This was a little out of my league. I finally concluded my search on a cooking show warning of new studies showing a possible link between Teflon and cancer. Great. Yet another thing to fear. I am officially going to bed now.

The next morning I brewed myself some green tea to ward off the cancer and made my way to my living room chair with my Bible. I happened to be in 2 Kings, chapter 17, when verse 33 arrested my attention, "They worshiped the LORD, but they also served their own gods." Verse 41 further compounded the description, "Even while these people were worshiping the LORD, they were serving their idols." God and gods: the people were living split lives, worshiping the One, while serving the others.

My mind instantly reeled back to the TV programs, representing the gods of money, lust, sex, and inordinate pleasure. I also considered the previous night's discussion that had been topically dense, full of questions and longings. Suddenly the Scripture sharpened the vagueness of our striving to a point. *Could it be that we are serving our own gods, though we sit on the front row of church and serve the fruit tea? Do we claim the Bible as our source of truth while our real counselors come from movie screens and magazines?* Perhaps so many of our struggles—lack of freedom, loss of spiritual desire, slavery to image, perfectionism, confusion, and infinitely more possibilities—have much to do with God *and* gods. The people in 2 Kings were worshiping God, but they were serving their idols.

In both verses it spoke of worship to God, but service to idols. An exquisite distinction divides the uses of the two words. For so much of my life I worshiped God: singing hymns, reading my Bible, confessing my belief in Him. Yet, if you could have witnessed what controlled me, you would see that in many cases it was my idols. Not carved images, but people, career paths, materialism, acceptance, and more. God (on some level) was getting my worship, but my gods were getting my service.

I believe this halfhearted living is possibly one of the reasons why so many of us have been stuck. Basically, we have edged God out. We have left Him with little room in our hearts. Our false gods have taken up our most treasured spaces, leaving little room for God to show Himself strong on our behalf.

After pondering these things further, it seemed that 2 Kings 17:33 was the seed from which our study needed to grow. Clearly this issue of false gods goes deep into each of our hearts. We had much to discover about this issue of idols, like, what do modern-day idols look like? Why are we serving them? How do we make them? How do we destroy them? Which ones are we serving? I'm so glad you're along on our journey. Lets get started with Bible study.

DAY 01 PERSONAL PHARAOHS
DEFINING OUR TERMS

Exodus 20:3
You shall have no
other gods before me.

False gods. Idols. Does any of this ring a Sunday School bell? I don't know if you had a background similar to mine, but I grew up in the church. (If you didn't, no worries, as you might actually have less baggage to sort through.) As with anything human, church always mingles the glorious with the flawed. Being in and out of so many things like church, youth group, and Christian school, one of the flawed elements for me was overexposure to certain words and phrases. Over time, these inherently good concepts either lost meaning through repetition, or became too connected with things like legalistic teachers or an organist with bad hair. (Have I mentioned the frozen lasagna?)

Terms like false gods or idols might have fallen into that kind of a category for you. Or maybe it's the other way around—you've had scarce exposure to those words, so instead of sounding churchy and rote, they may sound strange and cultish and make you want to run for something normal. Either way, I hope we find fresh meaning for old words and possibly new words for old meanings. Because anything taking the place of God in our lives deserves our attention—bad hair aside.

Considering our varied backgrounds and the possible connotations that go along with these terms, it's good to start by freshly defining them. Ponder this definition by Ken Sande:

> Most of us think of an idol as a statue of wood, stone, or metal worshiped by pagan people. ... In biblical terms, it is something other than God that we *set our heart on* (Luke 12:29; 1 Cor. 10:19), that motivates us (1 Cor. 4:5), that masters and rules us (Ps. 119:133; Eph. 5:5), or that we trust, fear, or serve (Isa. 42:17; Matt 6:24; Luke 12:4-5). ... An idol can also be referred to as a "false god" or a "functional god."[1]

What new thoughts does this definition bring to your understanding of a false god or idol?

When I consider what I set my heart on, what motivates me in life, what controls me, and what I serve with my energy and resources, suddenly I am far from graven images and am toe to toe with my lust for attention, my attachment to comfort, my demand for people to meet my needs. These are just a hint of the things I often look to as my personal saviors.

Look back at the definition and notice the term *functional god.* I especially like the use of this phrase because sometimes it's easier for me to determine what functions for me as a god as opposed to what is false. Also, I particularly like it because it puts an Old Testament concept in a current light. After discussing this concept with the girls, Alli sent us an e-mail that further explains:

Since I got home I've been thinking about what we talked about … Was thinking about that old boyfriend I mentioned, and just wanted to tell you how much it helped me to think about our definition of idols again. I started asking myself, "What about him was functioning as my god?"

The answer is that I would have done anything for him. He wasn't necessarily my motivation for everything, but I would have given up everything for him and done anything he asked. I was really that infatuated. Which by the way, the definition for that word is "an intense but short lived passion or admiration for." I thought that definition was perfect. God had someone more suited for both of us. It's amazing how gracious He is with us.

Anyway, just wanted to mention how much it helped me put things into perspective to remind myself of an idol as a "functional god."

Recently I've found myself fearful in relation to world affairs. The threat of terrorism, the reality of war, and the destructive wake of hurricanes have left me feeling vulnerable. Growing up I only saw these things as they related to other countries. Everything bad was "over there" someplace. Now such things float across the air in our backyard. It's made me realize something on a deeper level: I profess that my safety and security is in God, but the strength of America to protect me has in some ways functioned as my god.

Explain the difference between a professed god versus a functional god.

In my understanding, a professed god is who or what we say our god is; a functional god is who or what actually operates as our god.

Think of a few examples of functional gods in our society. Briefly list them below:

A professed god is who or what we say our god is; a functional god is who or what actually operates as our god.

Take a look at another great definition by Richard Keyes:

An idol is something within creation that is inflated to function as a substitute for God. All sorts of things are potential idols, depending only on our attitudes and actions toward them … Idolatry may not involve explicit denials of God's existence or character. It may well come in the form of an overattachment to something *that is, in itself, perfectly good* … An idol can be a physical object, a property, a person, an activity, a role, an institution, a hope, an image, an idea, a pleasure, a hero—anything that can substitute for God.[2] (emphasis added)

This definition really hits me. Not that I've never had affinities for things that were downright wrong or sinful, but most of my false gods have consisted of people or things that were—as Richard Keyes notes—in themselves, perfectly good.

As John Calvin put it, "The evil in our desire typically does not lie in what we want, but that we want it too much."[3] For me, this is far more characteristic of my own struggles with false gods.

Can you think of anything in your life that is inherently good and right, but that has become detrimental simply because you desire it too much? If so, explain.

Now that we've defined our terms, read Exodus 20:1-6.
What word does God use to describe Himself in verse 5?

A jealous God. Shows mercy to thousands who love God & keep commandments. Punishes for the sins of the fathers upon the children to the third & fourth generation of those who hate God

According to verse 2, do you think there is reason—apart from
God's pure power and sovereignty—for Him to be jealous?
If so, explain.

God was the only living God. He has a zeal for the truth that He alone is God.

Do you think it's significant that the very first commandment
God gave us is to have no other gods before Him? Explain.

This passage conforms to the pattern of ancient middle east treaties between a king and his servants. The Great King presented to His servants, the Israelites, the duties and obligations of the covenant He made with them.

I think the other nine commandments are virtually impossible to uphold
if we neglect the first commandment. If God is not God in our lives,
doesn't that make the rest of His commandments somewhat optional?
Just a thought.

Finish today by noting any penetrating or new realizations
you had. It can be anything—it doesn't necessarily have to
be a verse. Write it below.

DAY 02 PERSONAL PHARAOHS
NAMING OUR PHARAOHS

Yesterday we discussed some of the foundational elements of false gods: what they actually are and what they look like. Hopefully you already have a better handle on how these elements—that are substituting for God in our lives—might be entangling our souls. Perhaps you're already aware of something in your own life that has exalted itself to a position it was never meant to hold.

Right now I'm sitting in a room on the top floor of a hotel in Colorado. It's not exactly your four-star experience, mostly because I'm hearing incessant footsteps run back and forth across the ceiling. Birds, I'm imagining. Somehow they've made a nest between the drywall and the roof, racketing and rummaging at all hours. They're especially active at this moment, cooing and almost purring. I don't even want to know what's going on up there. It's annoying and a little gross really—rooming with birds. I'm actually wondering if they're here for the Internet access or what. Does the Ritz have birds? At any rate, they're not supposed to be here. Here on earth is fine, just not in the ceiling. So, as I'm writing about these false gods that aren't supposed to be housed in our lives I can't help but make the silly connection.

> **According to yesterday's definitions, write in your own words what a false god (functional god or idol) looks like today. Feel free to glance back to yesterday's study if necessary.**

To get a better handle on how our modern-day idols affect us, it helps to look into the past. First Corinthians 10:6-7 says the Old Testament accounts are examples so we will know how to live today. Oftentimes they are physical pictures that reflect spiritual principles. This week we will look at the false gods, captivity, and deliverance of the Israelites, while translating those physical examples onto a spiritual plane. Here's what I mean.

2 Kings 17:7-8
They worshiped other gods and followed the practices of the nations the LORD had driven out before them.

Read 2 Kings 17:7 and fill in the blank.

"All this took place because the Israelites had sinned against the LORD their God, who had brought them up out of Egypt from under the ___hand___ of Pharaoh king of Egypt. They worshiped other gods."

I have felt under the power of many things in my life. It could be as simple as not being able to pass up another cookie at dinner or as consuming as jealousy. For the Israelites, the controlling force was Pharaoh. Today, it might be alcohol, television, an unhealthy relationship, unforgiveness, or sexual addiction. As we read yesterday, it could also be something incredibly good that has only turned bad by virtue of how much it consumes you.

PERSONAL REFLECTION: Reflect on what currently holds power over you. Who or what is your pharaoh? Write it down. Be as detailed and specific as you can. You may have several—me too—but for now, focus on the one with the most power.

Keeping your own "pharaoh" in mind, read about the original Pharaoh and what his power looked like over the Israelites. Read slowly and thoughtfully and look for the specific ways the Israelites were oppressed: Exodus 1:1-22; 2:23; 3:7-10.

Taskmasters to afflict them, midwives told to kill male babies

Cite a few specific examples of how Pharaoh was oppressive.

He made them build store cities for himself.

Now list a few examples of how you are oppressed by the false god you wrote about above. Here's one of my personal examples to trigger your thinking: Early on in my career I was consumed by the success—or lack thereof—of my music. My happiness rose and fell on how many records I was selling and whether or not the record company was pushing my product. I missed many opportunities to relax and enjoy other aspects of life while trying to control my career. The deceiving element was that the more I tried to control it, the more it was controlling me. My satisfaction and identity were wrapped up in whether or not I was deemed a success. This was oppressive because it dictated my time, peace, happiness, and where my energies were directed. My career held all the power. It had become a god in my life. Achievement had become my pharaoh and it kept me anxious, self-centered, and generally discontented in life.

Your turn:

Today was mostly a time of personal reflection to identify the things that hold power over us. The false gods we serve hinder and hurt us in many ways, but it all starts with the power they hold. I wanted to go through the exercise of soul searching and describing our false gods because I believe this power can subtly control us without our knowledge. Socrates wisely said, "The unexamined life is not worth living," which is why I find today's exercises essential.

End by writing a prayer of acknowledgment. Tell the Lord about what holds you, oppresses you, and burdens you. Name your pharaoh to Him. Then, as stated in 2 Kings 17:7, ask Him to bring you out "from under the power" of whatever is holding you as we go through the next few weeks.

Your prayer:

> Achievement had become my pharaoh and it kept me anxious, self-centered, and generally discontented in life.

DAY 03 PERSONAL PHARAOHS
PURPOSEFUL PHARAOHS

2 Corinthians 1:9
This happened that
we might not rely on
ourselves but on God,
who raises the dead.

As I reflect on this week's topic, I remember the awful feeling of being under the power of someone or something. Lack of inward freedom is one of the most agonizing experiences of human existence. The one redeeming aspect is that blessings can grow out of our exasperating struggles with giants who are stronger than we are. I have been thoroughly changed, mostly for the good, from such bouts with weakness and powerlessness, even though it seemed unimaginable at the time.

If you need to, look back over yesterday's Scripture reading (Ex. 1:1-22; 2:23; 3:7-10) and answer the following question:

Besides crying out to God, what could the Israelites do about their situation?
☒ flee ❑ do nothing ❑ fight back ❑ hide

PERSONAL REFLECTION: Write about a time you felt absolutely powerless in a situation where all you could do was cry out to God.

Does the fact that the Israelites were powerless to free themselves from captivity encourage or discourage you as it relates to your own struggles?

The Apostle Paul faced similarly difficult situations. Check the way he described his hardships in 2 Corinthians 1:8-9.
❑ far beyond his ability to endure
❑ difficult, but manageable
☒ extremely hard, but nothing to be compared to his spiritual will

20

What reason did Paul give in verse 9 for his sufferings that were far beyond his ability to endure?

Persecution for speaking about Christ.

Both Paul and the Israelites were faced with situations totally beyond them. Those circumstances ultimately forced them to rely on God and not themselves. This gives me hope because I can't tell you the number of times I've uttered the words *I can't do this* or *I have no idea what to do.* Could this be exactly where God wants us, in order to show Himself strong on our behalf?

PERSONAL REFLECTION: Are you still relying on yourself to conquer your pharaoh? If so, explain.

If you're at the point where you have found yourself powerless and desire to rely on God, write it in a prayer below.

I want to close today by encouraging you in this: having freedom from our idols begins by recognizing our own powerlessness against them. Apart from the power of Christ, we are unable to extricate ourselves from their hold. This is good news if we can accept the truth of our own weakness while accepting the gift of His strength. He will do it.

Having freedom from our idols begins by recognizing our own powerlessness against them.

DAY 04 PERSONAL PHARAOHS
CREATING PHARAOHS

Isaiah 44:20
Is not this thing in
my right hand a lie?

I think the only thing worse than being under the control of something to no fault of my own is to be under the control of something I've actually created. It's pain with extra sides of guilt and regret.

Looking again at Exodus 1:8-11, was it the Israelites' fault that they found themselves in captivity? ☑ yes ❑ no

In this situation I think it's clear that the Israelites did nothing to deserve the torment they received from Pharaoh. This was not God's punishment. Disobedience is not mentioned. Their story is a healthy picture of good people who went through tremendous distress to no fault of their own. But this isn't always the case. Sometimes we set our own traps by creating our own gods. Isaiah 44:1-20 describes this scenario. At a first read this passage may seem archaic and out of touch, but I think the premise is actually quite modern.

Read Isaiah 44:1-20.
What did the people use to make their idols? List as many as you can find.

Metal, wood

What three types of people made these idols (vv. 11-13)?

Blacksmith Carpenter
Craftsman

Choose a word below that best describes the craftsmen, blacksmiths, and carpenters, collectively.
❑ tough   ☑ skilled   ❑ smart   ❑ brute

I find it interesting that the people who made these false gods were skilled professionals who used specific resources to make them, not the least of which was their own strength.

Do you think the fact that skilled craftsmen were used to make the people's idols applies to us today? If so, write your thoughts in the margin. How do we specialize in and use our resources on modern forms of idolatry? List a few examples that are pertinent to you on the next page.

People who are obsessed with body image might excessively work out, spend their time and money on workout equipment, pour over fitness magazines, count every calorie, talk disproportionately about physical image, and become extreme in their pursuit of diets and weight loss.

Of course nothing is wrong with being a carpenter, blacksmith, or craftsman. Nor is anything wrong with being fit and highly knowledgeable about health and muscle fitness. Certainly being skilled and wise are worthy and desirable goals. They become a problem when we use these things to create false gods that we end up serving.

> **In closing today, read 1 Corinthians 10:31: "Whether you eat or drink *or whatever you do,* do it all for the glory of God" (emphasis added).**

This verse gives us a litmus test for determining how our skills are being used. We can easily ask ourselves the question, *Am I doing this for God's glory, or for my own glory, pride, comfort, happiness, or other selfish motive?*

> **With this verse in mind, list your skills, talents, resources, passions, and areas of expertise below. After you've made your list, write about how each of these things can be used for the glory of God. As you're writing, mentally note where these things are misdirected or unfocused.**

> **Skills**   **How they glorify God**

> **Finish up with a moment of reflection before God. Ask Him to reveal to you if there is an area of your life you've been using for your own gain. If something comes to mind, write it below. Ask God to help you transform that energy, desire, or skill into what can be used for His glory.**

DAY 05 PERSONAL PHARAOHS
WHERE OUR HEART IS

Matthew 6:21
Where your treasure
is, there your heart
will be also.

The heart. It is possibly the most central part of our being. It guides, feels, listens, hurts, heals, dreams, loves, lives … It is not surprising that our gods would attach themselves there first. Or vice-versa. The idols in my life that have been the most difficult to root out—by far—have been the ones that I've let weave themselves deep into my heart.

Proverbs 4:23 gives wise instruction in this regard. What does it tell us to do?

Keep your heart will all diligence For out of it springs the issues of life

Above all else! *Above* all else. Above *all else* … above all else. Guard your heart. I believe God gives us these words because He created our heart to be the wellspring of life. And He knows that our gods go straight for the heart when looking for a place to erect themselves. When it comes to our theme of false gods, we have to start at the heart.

Enjoy the introspective nature of today, because it's vital for life change. Remember, we're walking together toward the goal of eradicating the things from our lives that are false, that lie, that kill, and that steal. But if we stop there, we miss the point: to make room for God to live unrivaled in our hearts, shedding life, light, glory, healing, holiness, miracles, peace, and more things than I could ever write.

Just for the sake of emphasis, write the words *make room* in the margin. It will be our two-word reminder of what we're ultimately "after" over the next eight weeks (and hopefully our lives).

Check out the nog blog
at: *http://www.
lifeway.com/
livingroomseries*

I recently wrote a song that expresses these sentiments. If you want to grab it off the Web site, feel free to listen and make it your own prayer. Or, just read it here if it suits you better.

FIRST IN MY HEART[4]

SO THIS IS LOVE, IT FEELS LIKE WAR
TO SLAY MY GODS BY THE SWORD
MAKING ROOM FOR YOU TO DWELL
HERE INSIDE OF ME UNRIVALED
THOUGH IT COSTS ME EVERYTHING
ONLY YOU WILL BE

CHORUS:
FIRST IN MY HEART, FIRST IN MY MIND
AND IN EVERYTHING I LONG FOR IN THIS LIFE
FIRST IN MY DREAMS, FIRST IN MY EYES
BEFORE EVERY OTHER LOVE THAT I DESIRE

SO SETTLE IN AND YOU NEVER MIND
THESE TREMBLING HANDS, THESE TEARY EYES
CAUSE I NEVER KNEW IT'D HURT SO BAD
TO TURN MY BACK UPON THIS GOLDEN CALF
LET ITS MEMORY FADE AWAY
TILL ONLY YOU REMAIN

CHORUS

TAKE THESE IDOLS A MILLION MILES
FROM THE ALLEGIANCE OF MY SOUL
FILL THIS HUNGER WITH YOUR WONDER
TILL ONLY YOU WILL, ONLY, ONLY, ONLY YOU WILL BE …

CHORUS

Today we'll look at only a few verses that are dense with soul-searching opportunities for all of us.

First, revisit Ken Sande's definition of an idol: "Most of us think of an idol as a statue of wood, stone, or metal worshiped by pagan people. … In biblical terms, it is something other than God that we set our heart on (Luke 12:29; 1 Cor. 10:19), that motivates us (1 Cor. 4:5), that masters and rules us (Ps. 119:133; Eph. 5:5), or that we trust, fear, or serve (Isa. 42:17; Matt 6:24; Luke 12:4-5). … An idol can also be referred to as a 'false god' or a 'functional god.'"[5]

Even though Sande doesn't use this word, I think we can almost sum up his definition by saying that what we *treasure* apart from God is where we find our idols.

Read Matthew 6:19-21. Where does verse 21 say our heart is?

*For where your treasure is,
There will your heart be also.*

Read Isaiah 44:9. Fill in the blank. The things they treasured were *useless*.

Read 2 Kings 17:15. We become like what we:

☒ follow ☐ reject ☐ worship ☐ wish for

Read all three verses again and sum up each one with a short sentence next to each reference:

Matthew 6:21 *Where you put your heart is where your treasure is*

Isaiah 44:9 *We follow our desires of our heart*

2 Kings 17:15 *When we reject God we follow idols.*

BELOW ARE MY OWN:

MATTHEW 6:21   WHAT WE TREASURE IS WHERE OUR HEART IS.

ISAIAH 44:9   IF WE TREASURE IDOLS, WE TREASURE WHAT IS WORTHLESS.

2 KINGS 17:15   WE BECOME LIKE WHAT WE WORSHIP/TREASURE.

As you look at your own life, which of the phrases above most catches your attention and why? Write several paragraphs. Be specific. Don't edit yourself. Just write.

Although each verse can have a sobering effect as we look at some of the worthless treasures of our lives, I want to consider the positive side as well. If God is our treasure, our heart will be there. If we treasure Him, we treasure what is of infinite value. If we worship Him, we will become like Him.

If we treasure Him, we treasure what is of infinite value. If we worship Him, we will become like Him.

Read 2 Corinthians 3:18. *We will be transformed into the same image as Christ.*

As I think of being transformed into His likeness, I am reminded of the positive meaning of becoming like what we worship. Looking at your own life again, ponder the ways you practically treasure the Lord and how you think those things have molded you into His image.

Creative Reflection: Go back to the verse that struck you as most profound—the one you wrote about before. Over the next few days ponder a song, movie clip, painting, picture, personal experience, example in nature, childhood remembrance, or anything (the sky's the limit) that best reflects that concept. Bring your thought to dinner next week. It's totally open ended; there's no right or wrong way to do it. Be creative.

1. Ken Sande, *The Peacemaker, Revised and Updated* (Grand Rapids: Baker Book House, 2006), 104.
2. Richard Keyes, "The Idol Factory" in *No God But God* (Chicago: Moody Press, 1992), 32-33.
3. C.J. Mahaney, *The Idol Factory* (Gaithersburg, MD: Sovereign Grace Ministries, 2001), 2.
4. "First In My Heart," words and music by Kelly Minter. Copyright 2007. ASCAP. Publishing: Minty Fresh Music.
5. Sande, 104.

BUTTERFINGER CAKE

PREHEAT OVEN TO 350° SERVES 16

1 box Devil's food cake mix
10 oz. cola or diet cola
1 egg white
7 oz. sweetened condensed milk
2 T. peanut butter
8 oz. frozen whipped topping (such as Cool Whip), thawed
7 Nestle fun-size Butterfinger candy bars

Combine cake mix, cola, and egg white. Bake according to cake mix instructions in a greased 9x13 pan.

A few minutes before the cake is to be done, combine sweetened condensed milk and peanut butter in a saucepan. Cook and stir on low to make creamy and warm.

When cake is done and still hot, poke holes in top of cake with a knife and pour peanut butter mixture over top of cake. You may have to spread the mixture a little to help it go down into the holes. Sprinkle top with half of the chopped Butterfingers. Cool cake completely.

Cover with Cool Whip and sprinkle remaining Butterfingers over top. Keep in fridge until ready to serve.

BLACK BEANS AND RICE
PREHEAT OVEN TO 325° SERVES 6—8

This is the meal we had the first time we all got together.
It's my New York friend's recipe. I hope you enjoy!

4 standard-sized cans of black beans
½ yellow onion
6 cloves garlic
1 bunch cilantro
8 oz. shredded Monterey Jack cheese
2 c. whole grain brown rice
2 avocados
1 jar salsa
1 c. sour cream
1 bag tortilla chips

Heat black beans in a pot over medium-high heat, keeping most of the juice. Chop onion and cilantro, mince garlic, and place all in a saucepan and sauté. After beans have heated for 20 minutes, stir the sautéed ingredients into the black beans. In a separate pot, begin preparing brown rice (follow instructions on bag). Pour black bean concoction into a 13x9 inch pan and add shredded cheese on top, covering extensively. Cover with aluminum foil and bake for 30 minutes at 325 degrees. Serve black bean entrée over the brown rice, having a nice spread of chips, slices of avocado, salsa, extra shredded cheese, and sour cream as toppings.

WHY IDOLS?
STEALING TIME

ALLI, LAURI, CARRIE, ANADARA, AND I GET TOGETHER ON MONDAYS.
IT WAS THE ONLY DAY THAT WORKED FOR ALL OF US. TODAY IS MONDAY. I WOKE UP THIS MORNING WITH GREAT INTENTIONS FOR OUR TIME TOGETHER TONIGHT. MY HOUSE WAS MOSTLY CLEAN, AND MOST OF MY ERRANDS HAD BEEN RUN. I HAD EVEN GONE TO THE DMV TO GET MY LICENSE RENEWED, WHICH I CONSIDER AN EXCESSIVE ACT OF EFFICIENCY ON MY PART. I WAS PLANNING ON GETTING TO THE GROCERY STORE IN THE MORNING TO PICK UP ITEMS FOR PASTA WITH HOMEMADE RED SAUCE. I HAD VISIONS OF THE SCENT OF SAUCE WAFTING THROUGH MY KITCHEN WHILE AUTUMN LEAVES FELL OUTSIDE MY WINDOW.
OF COURSE I WOULD BE ON MY COUCH WITH MY BIBLE IN HAND, CANDLE LIT, PUTTING FINISHING TOUCHES ON THE EVENING'S DEVOTION. I WOULD LEISURELY SET THE TABLE, TIDY UP LAST-MINUTE PILES, AND SET THE MOOD FOR THE GIRLS.

Enter reality: I woke up, was halfway into some sort of prayer and study when my phone rang … "Kel, can you help me out just a bit this morning. I'm in the studio today and I can't break away." It was one of those friends who had bailed me out too many times for me to say *I'm a little busy*. Turns out, all she needed was for me to deposit some checks and print out a document that needed to be overnighted. This was not going to be a problem.

Problem. The document was 176 pages long and the printer started rebelling at approximately page 84. At 85, it progressed to blinking and spewing paper. Alerts were popping up on the computer that didn't actually say, but clearly implied, *your day is hosed*. I thought about coaxing the printer through the next 92 pages, but when it kept telling me to insert new paper when it already had paper, I decided I would rather fight traffic and head to an office store than argue with an inanimate object.

So I got in my car with a darn good attitude, if I do say so myself. I was doing that positive self-talk (PST) thing where you remind yourself how God is in control and how thoroughly capable He is of handling the evening's dinner and study even if I'm a bit behind. During my PST, I saw a bank and decided to deposit my friend's checks. After doing so, I turned onto West End Avenue and was happy to be less than a mile from the place I could get this document printed and sent. I turned up my music—and it just so happened to be a CD of worship songs—so I sang along, praising God, probably making a bit of a scene. But that's not actually why the cop behind me started flashing his lights. Clearly this is a mistake. My tags have just been updated. I have my new license. I'm not speeding. My seatbelt is on. I'm not on the phone. And I'm singing worship songs! I was so perfect, I was almost bordering on annoying. This too was not why I was pulled over.

The policeman came to my window and took my license (the new one I just got). He asked me if I was aware of the fact that I had gone through a red light. I truly had no recollection. I didn't even remember a light, much less running it. So he took all the necessary information and went back to his car. Then I began that process of sitting, where you have nothing to do but stare while everyone drives by and gawks at you with relief and pity. Relief that it's not them, and pity because it's you. And then I sat some more. I just can't for the life of me figure out what they do back there for so long. Finally he returned with a ticket. PST came to a screeching halt.

Totally frustrated, I proceeded the next 200 yards and arrived at the office store, bustling in with my disk as fast as I could. It was now afternoon sometime and I was feeling the pressure of not being able to get everything done, along with the dread of driving school. Of course they said they couldn't have it ready for me right then; I would have to come by later and pick it up. So I left it and ran to the grocery store. That process actually went well. No eventful stories, just the fact that I was now in a fairly bad mood.

I threw the groceries in the back of my car—and I do mean threw—and raced back to pick up the document. Actually I didn't race. I desperately tried not to unconsciously run any more red lights, which is very hard to do because if it's unconscious, how do you know if you're doing it or not? I parked and ran into the store only to find a line of about ten people with very interesting and complex printing needs.

This triggered one of those irrational moments where you start having personal grievances against the people who want things like pictures blown up to banner sizes. *Seriously, what do they need that for?* I secretly mused. I found myself trying to supernaturally control the speed of the cashier, like if I thought hard enough and envisioned her moving just a little more efficiently, perhaps it would come true. I know this doesn't work, but I find it therapeutic anyway.

The seconds dragged by. I couldn't believe it. My heart was pounding and I could feel my veins constricting when suddenly I heard the man behind me say, "Wagamama?" I know this isn't very Christian, but I feigned oblivion. I knew he was referencing the shirt I was wearing that had that word on the back. He wasn't deterred. "Wagamama?" he repeated, this time louder.

I politely turned around. "It's a restaurant in London."

"London?" he replied. I nodded and faced forward.

"Can I ask you a question?" My body language was screaming no, but perhaps there was still some ounce of the Holy Spirit I had yet to quench that caused me to answer yes.

"What in the world are you doing over here when you live in London?" I should mention at this point that the man was speaking awkwardly loud, the line was barely moving, and it was now after 2:00 and I had virtually accomplished nothing.

"Actually, I live here. Just the shirt is from London." For some reason this really cracked him up. Chuckling he asked me, "Well what are you doing with a shirt from London when you live in Nashville?"

"A friend gave it to me," I quietly said, hoping he would tone his questions down a bit. Not so. He still wanted to know what kind of stuff Wagamama had and why they would sell clothing at a restaurant. I couldn't get to the counter fast enough.

Finally I got the document, slipped it in a package, and dropped it in the box. I got home, unloaded my groceries, chopped the produce, and got my sauce on the stove. I opened my Bible, attempting to gather myself and put the finishing touches on the study. The phone rang. It was my friend Kim.

"Kelly, Scott's been in a serious accident." Scott is one of my close friends who lives around the corner. My blood ran cold. "Is he okay?"

"He's actually doing fine, but the woman who hit him had to be cut out of her car and no one knows if she's even going to make it."

Stunned, I started pacing back and forth. Sensing I was not sure what to do next, Kim wisely suggested I drop everything and head to the hospital to see Scott and offer emotional support. I arrived moments later to a numb friend. Clearly he was shaken up by the experience, mostly concerned about the girl who had hit him. We eventually found out that she was stable and conscious;

that it was going to be a long road, but that recovery was probable. Scott insisted he was fine and suggested I get back to my house in time for our study.

I drove back, walked in the house at 5:50, and had a generous ten minutes before dinner was to start. Not having showered, having no make-up on, and being in my Wagamama t-shirt—which now carried bad connotations for me—were merely fringe issues. The dinner wasn't even close to ready, the table wasn't set, piles still lingered, and worst of all, I had no study prepared. Knock, knock. It was Carrie. She was early and I was grateful. I explained the situation to which she graciously grabbed a knife and started preparing the salad. Never had I seen someone cut tomatoes with such deftness. Lauri arrived next, also willing to help. She's a great cook and finds exceeding pleasure in watching me panic in the kitchen. It's not mean-spirited; it truly just delights her. Alli then sauntered in. She always seems so relaxed, so Bohemian with her Birkenstocks, jeans, and hoody. I profusely apologized for how harried I was and how late dinner would be. Alli just smiled, breathed an encouraging word, and tried to convince me that any of my hostess faux pas would be duly matched when we eventually met at her house. I doubted it. Anadara had gotten stuck in horrible traffic so she missed most of the drama; I missed her lovely strand of humor.

I suppose everything ended up okay in the end; it was just a lot more frenzied than I like. I think one of the things I learned was to get a little more prepared sooner—not to assume I'll have the afternoon to finish things up. Things will always crowd in. And they'll almost always take longer than we think. People will ask for favors, we will run red lights, strangers will crowd the store, and emergencies will occasionally surprise us. Some people say it's Satan, and maybe sometimes it is, but I think it's also just the way things go in life.

Even when you have these grandiose plans, spiritual plans nonetheless, things can unexpectedly turn. I suppose that's why I'm writing all this in regard to this week's homework, because there will always be a million nagging tugs on our time and attention, and somewhere in the middle of all the tugging it is essential we build a fortress wherein only God, His words, and our heart exist together for a time. It rarely happens accidentally.

This is a deeply important week in our series. Be intentional about your time with God, and guard it from nasty printers, traffic violations, and weird people in the checkout line.

DAY 01 WHY IDOLS?
IDENTITY

I really enjoyed my first week with the girls, though I'm finding out we're a little weirder than I originally thought we would be and I'm wondering if it's the same for you and your friends. I'm not sure when this started but we've begun to collectively refer to ourselves as the nogs—for "no other gods," of course. It's weird enough for adults to name themselves, but it's now taken on all kinds of grammatical forms as well—nogness, noggish, nogged, nogging. Anadara recently addressed us as nogarinas. It's nog-speak. I told you—weird. But we really like ourselves.

Alli just sent the following e-mail, which sheds a little light on the matter. Her header was: "Something you might find interesting …"

nog n. A wooden block built into a masonry wall to hold nails that support joinery structures. A wooden peg or pin.

At least we now know. What would we do without Alli?

Also, I don't know how the cooking is going for you. Some of us are better than others, but just so you feel better, the second time the nogs got together I burned a tray of pine nuts that filled my condo with 500 square feet of floating carbon particles. Yummmmm …

Last week we identified what idols are both broadly and personally. This week we'll look at the why of them. Why is it we choose them? Why are they appealing? Why are they so hard to resist? This is one of my favorite elements of our study because we get to uncloak the mystery of their allure. We get to unveil what our hearts are truly after. And all of this is important because if we can get at the why of idols, we can get at the root of them. Which is important so we can …

Write down our two words from day 5 of week 1 (p. 24):

making room

This is elemental, but continue the phrase. For whom are we making room?

God

Deuteronomy 7:6
The LORD your God has chosen you out of all the peoples on the face of the earth to be his people, his treasured possession.

The first two times the five of us met, we gathered for less of a study and more of a focus group. I was trying to figure out what was propelling us toward functional gods. Yesterday I had a similar meeting in Colorado Springs with a larger group. I asked the same questions. Interestingly enough I got the same answers. Almost verbatim.

One word I heard consistently was *identity*. It was a word our Nashville group had thrown out, and it truly surprised me, given that Alli, Lauri, Carrie, and Anadara are all married. For some reason, I thought identity was more of a single thing—not so much a universal thing.

I guess I've always had this wistful notion that if I were married I wouldn't struggle so much with who I am. But it seems that women everywhere are caught in an endless pursuit to discover their identity. And it's not just people in their twenties and early thirties. According to many of my friends who have lived just a little longer, finding identity can be a lifelong battle, a continuous cycle. Husbands don't seem to solve it. Kids apparently don't do it. Careers fall short—and I can speak directly to this one.

One of the great Christian clichés is that this problem is neatly solved when we find our identities in Christ. I agree. I also have never heard what exactly this means, how you do it, or what it looks like. But sometimes I think we don't know because we don't grapple with it on a core level. Today we'll explore a passage I hope will plunge us into the deep well of identifying our lives with Christ and what it actually looks like (and a lot of what it doesn't).

> **Read 1 Samuel 8:1-22. (It's been a few days, so I humbly remind you to read slowly. Meditate as you go.)**
>
> **According to verses 7 and 8, what were the people guilty of? Check all that apply.**
> ☒ **forsaking God**   ☒ **serving other gods**
> ❏ **having unholy feasts**   ❏ **not burning sacrifices**
>
> **What motivation led the people to desire a king (vv. 5,20)?**
> They wanted to be like other nations.

> Women everywhere are caught in an endless pursuit to discover their identity.

Name just a few things Samuel said would happen to them if they got their request for a king.

The king would take people's daughters and sons to be his servants, take their land, crops, livestock for his own

Talk about a bad list! Nothing good can come from it. Everyone is in big trouble if this list materializes. Yet the people wouldn't even listen to Samuel. Their minds were made up. With a blatant "no" they said, "We want a king over us." And the profound reason they wanted a king over them was so they could be like all the other nations.

Here's the curious part to me: The Israelites already had an identity. An amazing one at that—they were the chosen people of God! But as they began to forsake God and follow other gods, they lost sight of what they had and, most important, who they were.

Lauri just sent me an e-mail in regard to all this. I don't know if she wants this public or not, but I take great joy in sharing with you that she watches reruns of "The Cosby Show" and somehow made a connection to our study. By the way, have I mentioned how current our group is?

Hey you! I was just watching Cosby and I thought of you.

Denise had a boyfriend over for Cliff to meet for the first time. He said he wasn't going to college because he was going to spend his time "finding himself." Cliff asked, "Well, how long do you think that'll take?" He said, "Five to ten years." Cliff said, "Well, you'll be able to find yourself and several other people by that time." Later Denise said, "Well? Do you like him?"

Cliff said, "I don't know if that's him. He hasn't found himself yet."

Just had a laugh and thought you'd enjoy it too.

The only way the Israelites were going to "find themselves" was to realize that God had already found them— and that is everything.

What do Deuteronomy 7:6 and 14:2 say about their identity?

They were a chosen people, holy people, special treasure above all people.

Keep in mind those Old Testament verses while reading 1 Peter 2:9-12. *Chosen generation, royal priesthood, a holy nation.*

Through Christ, we are also the chosen people. We are part of the royalty of God. We are holy in His sight. We belong to Him. We have received mercy. This is our identity.

After reading these verses, which part of the description means the most to you?

Just to get a clearer picture of what all this actually looks like, what does Peter call the friends he's writing to in verse 11?

So journers and pilgrims

Strangers, aliens, peculiar people—as a kid, none of this sounded exciting to me. I would like to think I could run into the mall without people freezing in their tracks with looks of bewilderment at a Christian—without toddlers in their strollers crying, *Look, mommy, an alien buying shoes.*

Who wants to be a peculiar person? Somehow it was always the extremely out-of-touch individual who was elevated to a super-holy status because he had bad ties and polyester pants. Weird somehow meant holy.

But as I really look at this verse, I realize you have to keep going. Peter qualifies his statement in a way that transforms what sounds almost cult-like into a beautiful display of counterculturalism. In essence he is saying we will be strange and alien-like because our lives will stand out as so breathtakingly good in comparison with others. As a result those around us will want to glorify God.

The extreme goodness of our lives is the peculiar part. Goodness should be setting us apart in distinctive ways. Not a goodness that comes from self-righteousness or legalism, but goodness that is the fruit of obedience.

What does Peter say will obscure this goodness (v. 11)?

Fleshly lusts which war against your soul.

Fulfilling our sinful desires will snuff out this burning goodness. By indulging them we actually become the reverse of peculiar and strange. We become—hold your breath—normal. For those of us seeking individualism and distinctiveness, chasing our lusts will only make us like everyone else, with little identity at all.

Today we examined what finding our identity in a king (or anything else) looks like, and we also observed what finding our identity in Christ looks like. The former ended up being a mess for the Israelites. Saul was not a good god, nor a good identity to have. The latter picture we looked at is astounding to me. In fact—I'm nowhere near here—but I would love it said of my life: *The goodness of Jesus Christ burned so brightly in her that people glorified God; she almost seemed from another world.* This is the kind of stranger I want to be. I believe it's the kind of stranger Peter was referring to.

> **PERSONAL REFLECTION: What sinful desires are obscuring your identity in Christ? I don't want you to end on the negative, so after praying and naming those things, write how dealing with those sins could expose your God-given goodness and give you a greater identity in a world of hungry people.**

DAY 02 WHY IDOLS?
NEED

Genesis 16:11
The LORD has heard
of your misery.

Need. Many of us run to idols because we are convinced they will bring us what we need. Without further ado, read the story of Sarah and Hagar.

As you read Genesis 16:1-15, jot down any indications of gnawing needs you can detect in the characters.

The need to have a male child. Sarai was despised by her servants

When reading Scripture I am often most profoundly penetrated by small phrases. That's why I often encourage a slow reading of a text. I find that a pair of words can be more powerful than a quick read of an entire book. Chapter 16 houses an economy of words that are life-changing for me. One phrase was so impacting that I wrote the word *huge* in the margin next to it—but I'll get to that later.

According to verse 2, what was Sarah's perceived need?

To have a child through another person

You probably know that during the era in which Sarah and Hagar lived, the ability to bear children was essential. It was viewed as a need. If you weren't married and couldn't have children, you were basically seen as worthless in society. Speaking of identity, you had none.

What was Sarah's remedy to her problem? (Not God's, not necessarily Abram's)

Since she could not have children she told Abraham to take her servant.

Okay, so here's what I find amazing: Finish verse 2:"The LORD has kept me from having children. Go, sleep with my maidservant;
_____."

After the hundreds of times I've read this passage, never in my life have I considered Hagar an idol of Sarah's. Until tonight. Until I read the simple phrase, "Perhaps I can build a family through her." In those days it might as well have read, "Perhaps I can build a life through her."

In a way, this is staggering to me. Sarah was looking to an Egyptian slave girl to save her life. She was depending on someone she ended up hating. Just a passing thought—isn't it interesting that our false gods can even be the things we hate? Think of any kind of addiction.

Sarah's dependence on Hagar leads me to ask the obvious question: Other than God, who or what am I trying to build a life through? I think we've asked ourselves that question in this study a few different times in a few different ways. If you feel you have a new answer based on this reading, please write about it. But I want to take our personal reflection beyond identifying our Hagar. I want to take it to the next step, which I hope will be one of healing.

> **In getting to the Personal Reflection, describe a time when God was not showing up fast enough for you and you were convinced you had to fix things on your own.**

Read Genesis 21:1-6.

Here we get the end of the story—God's way. We saw what happened when Sarah tried to build her family through Hagar her own way. It was disastrous. Everyone was hurt in the process, not just Sarah. But here in Genesis 21 we see the fulfillment of God's plan, and this was going to happen with or without Hagar; with or without Ishmael; with or without Sarah's manipulation; with or without Abram's passiveness. But how nice if the story had simply been Isaac, without all the baggage.

How we complicate the process. I can't tell you how moved I was by this revelation last night, even on my cramped flight. God had this beautiful plan for Sarah in spite of how bleak things looked. Definitely she was in a bind. She had genuine cause for concern. But that's always going to be the place where our faith is tested. If it all looks easy and doable, it doesn't require faith.

Certainly Sarah had waited a long time for a "life." But God had fully intended to give that to her. Not through Hagar. Not through Abraham. Not through Sarah's scheming. But through Himself. And of course we know He fulfilled this promise in Isaac. This gives me great encouragement to wait for God and keep my feisty little mitts off the

Other than God, who or what am I trying to build a life through?

process. It doesn't mean I sit around. There's plenty to do. It just means I don't force the outcome.

PERSONAL REFLECTION: How does Sarah's story encourage you to wait for God's perfect timing and fulfillment in your own life?

This is a song I wrote with Margaret Becker called "Just Isaac." It packages a lot of what we looked at today and can be found on her record *Air*. Again, you can download it from the Web site, or just read below. As you reflect on the lyrics, consider praying that God would help keep you to the "Isaacs" of your life—that you wouldn't be lured to create "Ishmaels."

JUST ISAAC[1]
I COULDN'T BLAME HER FOR STRIVING
I'D DO THE SAME THING IF I WERE DRIVING
WITH A HALF VIEW AND A WILD TALE
DELIVERED BY AN ANGEL

I'VE BEEN SO TIRED FOR THE WAITING
THOUGHT I WAS CRAZY OR AT BEST MISTAKEN
AS THE SUN SET DOWN ON A THOUSAND NIGHTS
WITH EVERYONE A PIECE OF ME DIES FOR …

CHORUS:
JUST ISAAC, NOTHING MORE
JUST YOUR PROMISE AND NOT MY FORCED, CRUDE HANDS HELPING OUT
ADDING STUFF TILL IT CRASHES DOWN
JUST ISAAC, NOTHING MORE
JUST YOUR PROMISE AND NOT MY FORCED, MIXED BLESSINGS AND SURPRISES
WHEN EVERYTHING I EVER WANTED WAS JUST ISAAC

COMPLICATIONS AND ISHMAELS
WHY COULDN'T I BELIEVE THAT YOU'D BE FAITHFUL
THAT YOU'LL HAVE YOUR WAY, EITHER WAY
WITH ALL MY EXTRAS OR JUST PLAIN …

CHORUS

DAY 3 WHY IDOLS?
PAIN

Sitting at a restaurant across from a woman who works with troubled adolescents, I asked her, "What makes the people you counsel run to idols?" As we've looked at this week, we run to idols for identity. We run to idols out of need. Today we'll see our propensity to run to them out of the first answer she gave me: pain. But instead of finding someone who sought an idol in her pain, we'll look at someone whose pain drove her to God. Sometimes it's nice to look at the success stories.

First, a quote from Oprah I read in a magazine. She said: "My answer always comes back to self. There is no moving up and out into the world unless you are fully acquainted with who you are. You cannot move freely, speak freely, act freely, be free unless you are comfortable with yourself." [2]

Without denigrating the contributions of Oprah in any way, I cannot think of anything less satisfying, not to mention limiting, than having *myself* as the big answer to everything. You can be a success story and a billionaire with a worldwide audience and a mass amount of influence that genuinely helps people in significant ways, but if your answers are always coming back to self, there are only so many things you can do.

Mending a broken heart, saving a soul, or healing an incurable disease all fall outside the lines. Bearing a child—even with today's technology—is not always possible with the self alone.

> **Name something in your life that you would like to change but can't if left only to yourself.**

> **Hannah could relate. Read her story in 1 Samuel 1:1-28 and look for all the inferences of pain in her life.**

The Lord close her womb, Elkanah's other wife tormented Hannah and made her life miserable.

Hannah's obvious and foremost source of pain was her barrenness. But I think some lesser-discussed pains are important to note.

1 Samuel 1:27
The LORD has granted me what I asked of him.

I cannot think of anything less satisfying than having *myself* as the big answer to everything.

First off, Hannah's husband, Elkanah, had another wife named Peninnah, which is already a rocky start. Besides having children, what did Peninnah do to Hannah?

Torment her because she (Peninnah) had children and Hannah was barren.

Looking at verse 7, for how long did this go on?

many years

What state did Eli the priest think Hannah was in when he saw her praying in the Lord's house?

Eli thought she was drunk for her lips moved but she did not speak out loud

Hannah's pain list is mounting. She's sharing her husband. She can't bear any children. Her husband's other wife is provoking her and has the only thing she wants. The priest thinks she's drunk. Yet I see another problem of Hannah's. One much bigger than any of these. One much bigger than even the "self."

Who had closed Hannah's womb (vv. 5-6)?

The Lord

This was a great revelation to me a few months ago: In a sense, God was Hannah's biggest problem. It wasn't infertility, Peninnah, Elkanah, or Eli. For divine reasons, God chose to close Hannah's womb. It seems like a prime opportunity for Hannah to run to an idol for relief.

This might be a hard question, but why do you think there are times when God purposely brings pain into our lives?

44

The one thing we can always hold onto is that though He brings pain, it is always for our good. I almost want to hit myself as I write this, because it sounds so terribly patronizing and cliché, and I would just die if anyone read this the wrong way. But I'm at the point where I believe it and am having to live by it for everything it is. God has brought pain in my life. But as I have surrendered to it, He has used the flames of hurt to burn away the parts that need not linger. Good has been in His mind from the beginning. (I'm writing to myself right now.)

You've already read most of Hannah's story. If you're feeling ambitious, I would highly recommend reading her prayer in chapter two. But for now, I want you to ponder Hannah's life and answer this question.

> PERSONAL REFLECTION: How do you think Hannah was enriched by God's closing of her womb? (Of course, we can't miss the fact that He eventually brought her a son, Samuel. And we should all take note—without any baggage, unlike Sarah.)

DAY 04 WHY IDOLS?
SILENCE

Exodus 24:3
Everything the LORD
has said we will do.

Identity. Need. Pain. These are just a few of the catalysts behind our search for false gods. But what about something a little more abstract? Something that has less to do with us and more to do with God? What about God's silence? Often when the Lord is quiet, or when He's not acting on our behalf in the way we thought or hoped He would, we decide that we're on our own—that we need to look out for ourselves.

Read Exodus 24:12-18. What did Moses tell the elders to do while he was gone?
❑   prepare an altar for the Lord
❑   make alternate plans in case he didn't come back
☒   wait for him
❑   make a golden calf

How long was Moses up on the mountain (v. 18)?
40 days & 40 nights

Read Exodus 32:1. Why did the people seek a new god to go before them? *They said they did not know what became of Moses.*

In a sense, Moses was Israel's liaison to God. He would speak directly with the Lord and then pass on God's messages to the people. If Moses was out of pocket, it was almost as if God had disappeared for a time as well. Our experiences with God can be eerily similar. Throughout Scripture we see God silencing or removing Himself for a time for different purposes. Sometimes it was sin related, but often it had nothing to do with any wrongdoing on anyone's part; it was a test or a growth period for His children.

Just last year I went through a long season where God felt distant, if not gone completely. Though I don't believe He ever actually removes His presence from us, I do believe He deems certain times where we will feel as if His presence has been removed. These seasons tempt us to substitute tangible things that we can touch and feel for the God we temporarily can't sense.

Keep reading in Exodus 32:2-5. What did the Israelites do to remedy their situation?

❑ waited for Moses

❑ fasted for Moses to return

❑ asked Aaron to take Moses' place

☑ asked Aaron to make them gods

Where did Aaron get the gold to make the calf?

The earrings that were in everyone's ears

As is obvious, the people did not do what Moses had instructed the elders to do, which was wait for him to return. Instead, they got antsy and asked Aaron to make them new gods. Aaron used all their gold earrings to make the golden calf.

If you're at all speaking candidly with yourself, you might be thinking somewhere along the lines of *How dumb can you all be?* It seems almost ludicrous that they would actually say (my paraphrase), *By the way, this guy Moses who was sent by God to deliver us from the captivity of the Egyptians, who worked a bunch of miracles like turning water into blood, and who used his staff to part an entire sea so we could walk across it and then had it close up on the Egyptians—yeah, anyway, that was a little while ago and we haven't seen him for a few weeks, so we're wondering if you, Aaron, might be able to come up with something new for us.* It's easy to look at them and wonder how in the world they got there so fast. But I fear it's more relevant to our own lives than we care to admit. Look at this.

Go back in Exodus and read 12:35-36. Where did the Israelites get their gold earrings from to make the golden calf?

The Egyptians.

Who does it say made the Egyptians favorably disposed to give the Israelites that gold?

❑ Moses   ❑ Aaron   ☑ the Lord   ❑ They stole it.

Here's what's so penetrating to me about this: The Israelites turned God's gifts into gods.

The Israelites turned God's gifts into gods.

This actually melts my heart a bit. It elicits in me sadness for God when I think of how He gave such good and special gifts to His children and then watched them take those very gifts and turn them into objects of worship. This feels like a terrible yet common temptation and practice in modern-day life, as well as in my own life.

God had given them gold as earrings; they turned that same gold into a calf. The gold was the same, but the function changed. This reminds me of a definition we looked at last week that described how some of our false gods can be made of things that are in and of themselves perfectly good; they only become a problem when they take the place of God. The Israelites and the golden calf are such a fitting example of this.

As you go into closing prayer, consider A.W. Tozer's quote from the *The Pursuit of God*: "Sin has introduced complications and has made those very gifts of God a potential source of ruin to the soul."[3]

> **In closing, if this last section has been penetrating to you, spend some time in prayer discussing with God some of His gifts you have turned into false gods. Let Him lead you into putting them in their proper place and returning thanksgiving for what He has given. Write your prayer below if you wish.**

DAY 05 WHY IDOLS?
FEAR

I've been pondering something this week in regard to today's study: whether fear itself is an idol or the bond that attaches us to our idols. Initially I thought of fear as a definite false god because of its power to rule us, drive our decisions, and dictate our actions. Bottom line—fear motivates, therefore it must be an idol, or so I thought.

But I kept thinking … fear isn't something we want in our lives; no one likes to be afraid. It's unlike the gods of materialism, sex, power, and money, which bring us pleasure if only for a season. We don't seek after fear. To the contrary, we drown our fears with things like alcohol, escape, entertainment, and denial. For the most part, we're afraid of being afraid. So perhaps fear isn't a primary god but the guard that stands outside the castle where the primary god lives. In other terms, fear protects our idols. Here's what I mean: I have always been afraid of being abandoned. I'm not totally sure where this springs from, but the fear of being left alone is something I started fighting as a three-year-old, the day my mom dropped me off at pre-school. I was petrified. My heart was pounding, my hands were shaking, and all I wanted to do was get back in the car with my mom and go home. Not to mention that learning was low on my list at that point. I carried this fear of being left alone into my adulthood. If I'm not diligently guarding against it, I can allow others to control me because of my fear that if I don't do what they want, I will lose them and ultimately be left alone.

So here's the thing: In this situation my true idol is the security of people. Fear of not having this security is not necessarily the idol but is what secures me to my idol. I think if we can separate our fear from our idols it will help us think more clearly and deeply about what is actually ruling us, and how fear is the agent hired by our idols to keep us attached.

If I'm losing you, my condensed version is this: Whatever we fear is our god. Fear itself is not the god; the object of our fear is the god.

Joshua 1:9
Have I not commanded you? Be strong and courageous. Do not be terrified; do not be discouraged, for the LORD your God will be with you wherever you go.

Fear itself is not the god; the object of our fear is the god.

How does fear play into one of your main functional gods?

Are you afraid to leave this idol behind? ❑ yes ❑ no
If so, of what are you afraid?

At least in my own life, fear has been the single most debilitating and paralyzing emotion I've experienced. Ever since I had the ability to formulate thoughts, I was fearful. I was afraid of being away from my parents, afraid to go to school, afraid to ride the bus, afraid of a tornado blowing our house apart, afraid of the Nazis coming to America and putting all the Christians in prison camps. As I've grown up, my fears have grown up. They're a little more adult, a little bigger in magnitude. (Well, not bigger than the Nazis, but you understand.)

In all this, I will say that Scripture has been tremendously effective in combatting my fears. Not because Scripture is full of helpful quotes about how not to be afraid, but because it is actually the recording of God's heart toward His creation—a creation He knows is prone to be afraid at every turn. He knows our frailty. He knows what causes our blood to run cold. He knows that fear can be our default. I wonder if this is why Scripture has so much to say about it.

Here are some verses from both the Old and New Testaments. They represent a mere slice of the passages that deal with fear, but these few address an assortment of fears. Do a cursory reading of each verse while being sensitive to the one (or few) that touch you most. (I know it looks like a lot, but hang with it— it will go faster than you think.) Circle the references that particularly move you.

Joshua 1:9	Isaiah 8:11-13	John 6:20
Psalm 56:3	Isaiah 44:8	John 14:27
Psalm 56:4	Isaiah 51:12	Acts 18:9
Psalm 91:5	Jeremiah 1:8	1 Peter 3:14
Psalm 112:7	Jeremiah 39:17	1 John 4:18
Psalm 118:6	Matthew 17:7	
Proverbs 3:24	Mark 5:36	

Go back and look at the verse(s) that meant the most to you. Write, in your own words, their meaning and how they relate to your personal fears.

"Have I not commanded you? Be strong and of good courage, do not be afraid, nor be dismayed, for the Lord your God is with you wherever you go." Joshua 1:9

End today's time by praying the truths you found in Scripture. Verbalize the truth out loud if you can.

"Do not fear, nor be afraid. Have I not told you from that time and declared it? You are my witnesses. Is there a God besides me? Indeed there is No other Rock I know not one." Isaiah 44:8

Be at peace today. Know that If God tells us not to fear, He will empower us not to fear. Cast your burdens before Him. Pour out Your heart. He is near.

Do not be afraid of sudden terror, nor of trouble 3:25

"When you lie down, you will not be afraid, yes you will lie down and your sleep will be sweet." Proverbs 3:24

1. Written by Margaret Becker and Kelly Minter, Copyright 2007. Modern M Music, Admin. Music Services, (SESAC), Minty Fresh Music (ASCAP).
2. "How I Got There," *Newsweek*, October 24, 2005, 48.
3. A.W. Tozer, *The Pursuit of God* (Camp Hill, PA: Christian Publications, 1993), 21.

BECKER'S PASTA
SERVES 4 GENEROUSLY

One of my all-time favorite meals, indeed! You will never stop pulling this one out, I promise.

1 lb. boneless, skinless chicken breasts
1 lb. bowtie pasta
2 pkg. sun-dried tomatoes, softened according to package instructions and cut into strips
1 garlic head
1 can of pitted black olives, chopped
16 oz. feta cheese, crumbled
½ c. pine nuts, toasted

Slice chicken in bite-sized pieces and sauté with sun-dried tomatoes and minced garlic until the chicken is cooked through. Cook pasta according to package directions. In a large bowl, mix crumbled feta, pine nuts, and chopped olives. After the chicken, sun-dried tomatoes, and garlic have been sautéed, add them into the bowl of dry ingredients and toss thoroughly. When pasta is cooked, add it to the mixing bowl and toss again. The pasta is then ready to serve.

bread and dipping oil
Get a fresh round loaf of your favorite bread (sourdough, Italian, French are all good). In a dipping bowl, pour in extra virgin olive oil and add balsamic vinegar, cracking fresh pepper and salt over top. Finish off with fresh Parmesan or Romano cheese.

CAPRESE SALAD
SERVES 4

4 vine-ripened tomatoes
8 oz. fresh mozzarella cheese (preferably the kind packaged in water)
basil leaves
fresh cracked pepper
salt
olive oil
balsamic vinegar

Slice tomatoes (approximately four slices per tomato) and slice fresh mozzarella (unless you bought the small balls, in which case, leave them as is). Wash basil and layer tomato slice, mozzarella slice, and basil leaf, repeating this pattern until you are through your ingredients. You can be as creative as you want with the presentation. This is merely one suggestion. After layering, sprinkle salt and pepper on salad. If possible, salt the tomatoes as this will bring out their flavor. After sprinkling the salt and pepper to taste, drizzle olive oil and balsamic vinegar over the salad.

I'VE BEEN RUNNING FOR AS LONG AS I CAN REMEMBER.
I MEAN, NOT RUNNING FROM STUFF, JUST RUNNING FOR EXERCISE AND EMOTIONAL STABILITY. AROUND THE AGE OF 10 I DISCOVERED A ONE-MILE CIRCULAR ROUTE THROUGH THE NEIGHBORHOOD THAT I TRAINED MYSELF TO COMPLETE WITHOUT STOPPING (BIG STUFF). AT AGE 12 I JOINED THE LOCAL TRACK TEAM. IN HIGH SCHOOL I RAN AS PART OF MY REGULAR WORKOUTS FOR BASKETBALL AND SOFTBALL. BY COLLEGE IT HAD BECOME PART OF MY LIFESTYLE.

The bad news about this insignificant trivia is that I am not a good runner nor do I like it. I'm not good at it primarily because I'm slow, have little endurance, and have never experienced that thing that annoying people refer to as a "runner's high." Is it too much to ask for just one endorphin? And why is it that all the other joggers who pass me on the streets look as if they've escaped the law of gravity? They bounce down the road as if they are out for their morning jog on the moon. I, on the other hand, feel like I have a small child on my back—but only when I go out to run. It's really weird.

I guess the good news is that it's possible to stick with things you don't like and aren't particularly great at, because I am in my twentieth year of fairly regular runs. I've found that running helps my mental outlook considerably. I can fritter away an entire day—which I desperately try not to do often—and can still feel like I've accomplished something significant if I've kept my legs moving faster than a walk's pace for anything more than 25 minutes. I like the fact that I can get outside, breathe the fresh air, hear the church bells ring (I *do* live in the South), pass the kids on the play-ground, feel the breeze, and after all that, arrive back at my doorstep with legs that are just a little bit firmer than before. I also love the feeling of being depleted of excess energy. It's a good exhaustion, one that makes me feel more relaxed and helps me sleep better at night.

Last week I was out for one of my neighborhood runs on an exceptionally hot and humid day in Nashville. Stifling is the word that comes to mind. I was about 20 minutes into my route when I noticed the oddest thing on the sidewalk. At first glance it looked like a dead baby alligator, except I

know we don't have alligators in Nashville, so I downgraded my assessment to a lizard of some sort. It was at least nine inches long and had very sizeable legs like it could have been someone's pet iguana that had escaped from its cage. Or … maybe it really was just a plain Nashville lizard. I'm just not educated in these areas.

The really bizarre thing—and the thing that incidentally has to do with this book—is that its head was stuck in a Dr. Pepper can. I am not making this up. I have several theories, but my best one is that the glistening drops of sugary water lured this reptile in on a hot summer's day. The poor little thing had worked so hard to wedge its head in there that it couldn't get it out. It suffocated in the smothering heat.

The reason I know all this is because I picked up the end of the mildly-crushed can to see its head, and its body just hung there. I was a little grossed out but still happy for the running break. It sort of brought me back to my younger years of hunting for frogs and snakes in the creek behind our house. I was always the one who led the charge in finding these creatures, but I was way too fearful to actually handle them. Kind of the same thing here except I had to act a little more adult in case a bouncing runner came by.

And, because I'm a little older now and these things hit me more metaphorically, I couldn't help but catch the symbolism. As I stood there staring at this peculiar sight, I thought of the many times I had discovered a few drops I thought were sure to offer life. They were sugary sweet and went down smoothly, offering a respite from the blaze of summer's heat. These experiences were the pinnacle of everything that encompassed the word life for me. Or were they? Sadly—and I do mean very, very sadly—in the end they left me more thirsty and desperate than before, craving what could never satisfy.

I suppose the most frustrating thing is that a million Dr. Pepper cans along the way tempt us with their seemingly immediate ability to quench our thirst. I recall the many situations where I wedged myself into something I just knew would bring relief from the scorching heat, but it left me suffocating instead. How easy these places were to walk into but nearly impossible to back out of. The lizard and the Dr. Pepper can spoke to me of something universal that none of us can escape: a desire for refuge, a need for relief, water for our hearts and souls. The tricky part is where we find this sanctuary and how we choose to satisfy our needs. His was a deathtrap. A deceptive offer. A lie.

From everything I understand Scripture to reveal, I believe only one source of satisfaction and refuge exists. Not one manifestation, but one source: "Every good and perfect gift is from above, coming down from the Father of the heavenly lights" (Jas. 1:17). God is the author of all good gifts—relationships, food, pleasures, family, summer night skies, melodies, and a million other graces. He uses a colorful palette to satisfy, though none as great as Himself. In Genesis 15:1, God comforted and blessed Abram by telling him, "I am … your very great reward." Verse 2 always strikes me as oddly humorous when Abram responded, "O Sovereign LORD, what can you give me?"

In essence Abram said, "I'm glad You're my reward, but seriously now, what are you going to give me?" Well, God did that too. He said He would bless Abram with children and make him into a great nation, but He began by revealing Himself as fully sufficient apart from what He offered.

God is teaching me this lesson, too. I am in the process of understanding the immense reward of God. Simply God. Apart from all He can do or give. But when it comes to His gifts, I am progressing in my ability to discern between all that He has given me as provision and the ever-seducing sugary drops. I am learning not to believe the lies. They have devastated me too profoundly for me not to take note. Notes that actually began in the garden of Eden amidst a curious woman, a serpent, and a piece of fruit. What was the lure? What was the lie? What was the cost? These are just a few of the questions I want to ponder with you, not for the sake of academics, but for the sake of life. All this from a lizard and a Dr. Pepper.

DAY 01 LIES
BEHIND EVERY FALSE GOD IS A LIE

Genesis 3:1
Did God really
say …?

Behind every false god is a lie. I suppose that's the reason they're false. Though seemingly obvious, understanding this is fundamental to dismantling our idols. We are in the process of taking our idols apart to make room for God. He will be God whether we make room or not, but how much we miss if we do not allow Him full space in our hearts! Second Chronicles 16:9 says, "The eyes of the LORD range throughout the earth to strengthen those whose hearts are fully committed to him."

I just got back from the dentist. I have turned over a new leaf with the whole dental care thing and have been religious about twice-a-year visits, earnestly hoping this would cut down on my overall dentistry bills. So far my plan has not worked as I'd hoped, evidenced by the $712.00 bill they gave me along with my "free" floss and toothbrush.

As if the whole expensive experience was not enough, I got the pleasure of watching some show during my cleaning about a researcher who had studied how to match people up with jeans that would make their behinds look better. Apparently there was an entire science to this, one which the woman being interviewed had researched for years. And this was not cable either. It was the 12:00 news. *Is nothing sacred anymore?* I thought with my mouth jarred open—drooling, I'm sure. Is not even the dentist's chair safe from the din of the media's view of how we should look in our pants?

Besides the stress of how expensive it is to keep my teeth clean, I left with the awareness of how difficult it is to live in America. No question, we are blessed on virtually every front, from wealth to medicine to education to freedom. But we're at a significant disadvantage when it comes to the barrage of information society and the media continually propagate—even while getting our teeth cleaned. We are constantly bombarded with what is sure to make us "happy" and "satisfied." (Although it rarely feels like bombardment—that would be too easy to discern!) It feels alluring and promising, packaged in glossy magazines and inviting commercials, on gripping sitcoms and in melodic pop songs, on the bodies of models and even in the words of friends.

I don't know how to fashionably state this except to say that we are being lied to every day, and greater still, we are being deceived by those lies. After all, false gods are named so for a reason: behind every good lowercase god is something false, otherwise I guess they would be called something different. But the problem resides in the fact that we don't recognize the lie. Instead we buy straight into the god for all it promises us. On the surface it all seems to make so much sense. These arguments made similar sense to Eve, proving a precursor to our own struggles with deceit.

Today we're going to focus on a very small portion of Scripture, but I pray you can dig a lot out of it. Read Genesis 3:1-6.

Looking at verse 6, what three things attracted Eve to the fruit?

Looked good, pleasant to the eyes, good for food, and desirable to make one wise.

Before we go further into this, I have to confess that I have been horribly deceived at different times in my life. Verse 6 is so personal to me because I, like Eve, have talked myself into things that later brought so much pain. It helps me to see how she got there.

First off, Eve saw that the fruit of the tree was "good for food." After reading Genesis 1:29 and 2:16-17, why does this first reason seem like an insufficient justification?

God had already given all the other tree and their fruits. God commanded Adam & Eve not to eat of the fruit of the tree of knowledge.

After buying my own place, I have become a helpless slave to visually-pleasing environments. I rarely have the money to keep up with my eye, but color, textures, lighting, and art have stolen my affections for better or worse. So I really get this next motivation that propelled Eve a breath closer to her monumental bite … it was "pleasing to the eye."

I can easily get there! Place me right in the middle of the garden where an angelic devil whispers sweetly in my ear while that piece of fruit shimmers in the sunlight, and my choice sadly becomes the same as Eve's.

Place me right in the middle of the garden where an angelic devil whispers sweetly in my ear while that piece of fruit shimmers in the sunlight, and my choice sadly becomes the same as Eve's.

The media know the power of "pleasing to the eye." What are some ways commercials, television, or magazines try to appeal to our eyes?

They tell us we must have this and we need this, and we will look so good in it or on it.

The last of Eve's three convincing reasons was that she believed the fruit to be "desirable for gaining wisdom." The King James says, "To make one wise." Can you think of something that attracted you based on the wisdom you could gain? Before answering the question, look at the Hebrew definition of the word *wise* here: "to be prudent, be circumspect, wisely understand, prosper."

This is not a totally black and white exercise, but generally speaking, answer the following (check all that apply):

1. "Good for food" is primarily about meeting Eve's _____ needs.
   ❏ mental ❏ emotional ☒ physical ❏ spiritual

2. "Pleasing to the eye" is more about meeting her _____ needs.
   ☒ mental ☒ emotional ❏ physical ❏ spiritual

3. "Desirable for gaining wisdom" is about meeting her _____ needs.
   ☒ mental ❏ emotional ❏ physical ☒ spiritual

Eve perceived this fruit to offer satisfaction to an array of needs: mental, physical, emotional, and even arguably spiritual. Yet the fruit provided none of what she had hoped for and everything she would have desperately wanted to avoid.

PERSONAL REFLECTION: Eve was deceived. Pulling her experience out of the garden and into modern-day life, how does her story parallel your own vulnerability to being similarly deceived?

DAY 02 LIES
BEHIND EVERY FALSE GOD IS DECEIT

===================================

I want to pick up right where we left off yesterday. From memory, can you list the three things that attracted Eve to the fruit on the tree of the knowledge of good and evil? (The answers are found in Genesis 3:6.)

1 Timothy 2:14
It was the
woman who was
deceived.

I've read this passage countless times, yet something very interesting struck me recently. I'm hoping it will be as intriguing to you.

Looking at the three reasons above, circle the ones that are true. For example, if you think the fruit was good for food, circle it. Do the same with two and three.

How many did you circle? _____

I'm not totally convinced we know the answer, but I'm going to argue that all three are true. Here's why. I think the fruit could be eaten and was nourishing. After all, when Adam and Eve both ate of it, neither died of poisoning, nor is there any mention of them getting sick. As far as "pleasing to the eye," it's pretty straightforward. Eve saw the fruit and thought it looked quite good.

Now, "desirable for gaining wisdom" is the piece that's a little cloudier, but we'll get there in a moment. First, read Genesis 3:4-5. What are the three things Satan argues in these verses? Fill in the blanks.

1. **You will not surely** _die_ **.**

2. **For God knows that when you eat of it your eyes will be** ___opened___ **,**

3. **And you will be like** ___God___ **, knowing good and evil.**

According to Genesis 3:7 and 3:22, were Satan's statements true? ☐ yes ☐ no ☒ some

Satan seems to have told them nothing but what was true. They did not physically fall over dead. Their eyes were indeed opened and they became like God in the sense that they now knew good and evil.

> **Given that the knowledge of good and evil is a type of wisdom, would you feel comfortable circling "desirable for gaining wisdom" as being true about Eve's perception of the fruit?**
> ☒ yes ☐ no

Okay, let me summarize thus far what is highly intriguing to me: I haven't found any lies! Is anyone else puzzled?

> **Look at 1 Timothy 2:13-14. What does it say about Eve?**
>
> **It was the woman who was** _deceived_.

Deception is very, well … deceiving. Michael Wells of Abiding Life Ministries says one of the most profound things: "Satan will tell us what's true, but he never tells us the truth." Let that sink in for a moment. If you're currently struggling with your finances, you might think something along these lines … *I don't have enough money to pay my bills this month; I'm going to lose everything.* It might be true that you don't have enough money to pay your bills, but the truth is that God will take care of your every need (see Matt. 6:25-30).

Or, here's another one … *My boyfriend/husband has rejected me; I will never be loved.* It might be true that you have been rejected and abandoned by someone you loved, but it is not the truth that you will never be loved, for God absolutely will not forsake us or withdraw His love (see Deut. 31:6).

I'm sure you can see the pattern here. I think this is what we see in Genesis 3. Satan spoke a lot of true things, yet none of it was the truth! This is where deception plays such a huge role in our lives. Though we all have succumbed to believing bold-faced lies, my hunch is that we have far more often been captivated by sheer deception.

> **Write in your own words what you think the difference is between a lie and deception.**

Going back to Genesis 3, I think it's so important to note all that was lost on that very day. Though I don't believe we will ever fully know all the ramifications, we know a few things for sure.

First off, sin entered the world. We were moved from a perfect garden to a fallen world. Our relationship with God was broken. We suddenly knew both good and evil, and I don't believe we were ever intended to house such knowledge. In fact, I don't believe we have the capacity for this knowledge and yet we are forced to carry it. This is a form of wisdom we were never intended to have. Our eyes were opened in extremely harmful and painful ways (for example, suddenly Adam and Eve were aware of their nakedness). And, yes, we did die. Not immediately, but everyone born on earth eventually dies—there are no exceptions.

Now see, this is the truth! What Satan told them was true didn't hold a candle to what God told them was truth.

> **PERSONAL REFLECTION: I** am hoping you can personalize this information in a profound way. Write about a situation in which you are (or have been) struggling between what is true and the truth. Keep in mind that circumstances often present things that are "true," but God's Word always presents truth.

> **I want to end by having you meditate on the truth of what God told Adam and Eve in the garden. Read Genesis 2:15-17.**

When we stray from God's original words to us, it becomes amazingly easy to get caught up in deception and counterfeit options. I have heard that people who need to recognize counterfeit money train by studying the original. Teaching them what a million possible counterfeits look like makes no sense when all they need to know is the real thing.

If Eve had just stuck with Genesis 2:16-17 she would have never needed to go through chapter 3. I pray the same for us. In order to stick with the truth, we have to know it.

What Satan told them was true didn't hold a candle to what God told them was truth.

DAY 03 LIES
BEHIND EVERY FALSE GOD IS INTIMIDATION

2 Chronicles 32:8
With him is only the arm of flesh, but with us is the LORD our God to help us and to fight our battles.

I have a friend who's a single missionary in China. I can't think of anything I'd be less cut out for, and yet when she looks at my terribly transitional, busy, often lonely, traveling life in the United States, I think her sentiments for my work are the same. Just today I got an e-mail from her in regard to a few months she recently spent in the States. She had the opportunity to stay with several people and get a glimpse into their lives, and this is what she had to say:

If it be any encouragement to you all, this is what I saw, especially in America: pain (deep, private, unanticipated, suffocating) met with stubborn hope (white-knuckled clinging to Him, rock-bottom conviction that His offer of Reconciliation is the only viable option, and a willingness to risk believing that Redemption is not only something that means we get to go to heaven, but something that He is passionate to carry out now, in specific life situations, to make things show His brand of beauty—in which a healed relationship or person can reflect more glory than one who never knew brokenness).

I wonder if that describes anyone involved in this study? People who are clinging to God with fierce abandon despite their caving and pained hearts, believing indeed that "redemption is not only something that means we get to go to heaven, but something that He is passionate to carry out now." Functional gods will not offer this redemption. The lies that circle our false gods like buzzards will try to convince us that redemption is wrapped up in our idols, but it will never be so.

Today we're going to look at an Old Testament account of truth and lies colliding in front of the people of Jerusalem—it's one of the most clear-cut examples in Scripture I know. Today, as you're fighting to tell yourself the truth, I hope you're encouraged by this account.

> **Read 2 Chronicles 32:1-23. Be looking for all the statements of truth and all the statements attacking the truth.**

> **What did Hezekiah promise the military officers in verses 7-8?**

With us the Lord our God, to help us and to fight our battles.

How do John 16:33 and 1 John 4:4 amplify Hezekiah's words in 2 Chronicles?

The Lord overcomes the world
He who is in you is greater than he who is in the world.

PERSONAL REFLECTION: **How do these verses encourage you as you look at the challenges you face? Meditate on how these truths would affect your circumstances if you really believed them.**

Look back at verses 10-19 of 2 Chronicles 32. What were some of Sennacherib's tactics against the Israelites?

Told them no god from any nation was able to deliver them from his hand.

One of Sennacherib's phrases in verse 10 caught my attention: "On what are you basing your confidence, that you remain in Jerusalem under siege?" I can think of a few times in my life when I have chosen to "remain under siege" because I believed that God wanted me right where I was. It could be a troubling job, a difficult marriage, an uncomfortable home. Regardless of the circumstances, it takes confidence to believe that God is going to protect and take care of us as we wait in difficult situations. I find it interesting that Sennacherib went straight to the root of their confidence in God by trying to question it. It reminds me a lot of Satan coming to Eve in the garden and asking, "Did God really say …?"

> Regardless of the circumstances, it takes confidence to believe that God is going to protect and take care of us as we wait in difficult situations.

Last week when the girls and I met, Carrie mentioned that one of the primary issues she deals with in regard to lies is, "Did I really hear God right when He said …?" I think this is exactly what Sennacherib was going for in this situation. He wanted the Israelites to question their God and their sanity, to wonder if they really heard Hezekiah correctly.

PERSONAL REFLECTION: With what strategy of Sennacherib's can you most closely identify when you think of the ways the world or Satan comes at you with lies? Write about the example you see in 2 Chronicles and how that practically plays out in your life.

What kind of king had Hezekiah been (2 Chron. 31:20-21)?

He prayed and did what was good and right before the Lord his God.

Now look back at verse 1 of chapter 32. What happened?

The king of Assyria came to Judah to win them over to himself.

Closing thought: What does this tell you about obedient people who go through trials?

We all go through trials and trust God for He will be with us.

Be encouraged if you find yourself in a difficult time, though you have been seeking God. It says that Hezekiah had been faithful, yet he was being attacked. I take heart that God proved Himself greater than the empty threats and attacks of Sennacherib. I pray we will find God personally greater than the Sennacheribs in our own lives and circumstances. Amen.

DAY 04 LIES
BEHIND EVERY FALSE GOD IS A DOOR WE'VE LEFT OPEN

I strongly believe that what we read, watch, and listen to have a profound effect on us, and I've been personally convicted of this in my own life. Most of us have our secret indulgences when it comes to magazines, television, music, and movies. For me, they usually follow thoughts like, *I don't agree with everything in this, but it has an over-all good message. This is so brainless it can't hurt. It's just so stupid it's funny. I don't really care about this stuff, but it's kind of interesting. It's just brain candy.* Or maybe you've never really thought about what you watch, read, or listen to, much less how it affects you.

When it comes to lies, I can't help but think of how often we're exposed to them from media and culture. So much that is portrayed to us is riddled with lies; but they are friendly ones, attractive ones, and seemingly innocuous ones. Many of them are so subtle we no longer detect them, and the ones that are glaring and huge we dismiss as things we believe don't affect us.

I know … you're scrambling for anything else to do but read further. I know no fashionable way to treat this, but before you totally shut down, I'll say that I am not coming from the angle that the TV is from the Devil and Hollywood is from hell. I don't see God's heart in Scripture telling us to separate ourselves with a self-righteous finger that points at all the "sinners" in pop culture. Instead God clearly teaches us to love all people. But loving is very different from putting ourselves in the way of messages that oppose His truth. It's different than leaving open doors for the lies of culture to waltz into our hearts. (Psalm 1:1-2 comes to mind.) This will hopefully become clearer as we go on in today's study.

> **Read 2 Timothy 3:1-16. How do you see the characteristics in verses 1-5 being portrayed specifically in media today?**

Unthankful, unholy, unloving, unforgiving, slanders, no self control, brutal, traitors, haughty, lovers of pleasure

> **According to verse 6, how do these people and their beliefs make their way into our homes?**

They creep & make captive.

Romans 16:19
I want you to be wise about what is good, and innocent about what is evil.

Blessed is the man who does not walk in the counsel of the wicked or stand in the way of sinners or sit in the seat of mockers. But his delight is in the law of the LORD, and on his law he meditates day and night (Ps. 1:1-2).

Verse 13 says that these types of people will go from bad to worse, _deceiving & being deceived._ (fill in the blank).

What does the very end of verse 5 say?

And from ~~this~~ such people turn away

Your Take: What do think this means?

Most of us are not out choosing friends who are slanderous, self-absorbed, abusive, conceited, and disrespectful, but perhaps these traits are "creeping" (KJV) into our lives during prime time, at the movies, in our favorite magazines, and on our iPods.

I know of no pleasant way to address today's theme, for no one wants to part with their media "comfort foods." It's as hard for me as it is for anyone, but I've found that cutting certain programs and reading materials out of my life have made huge differences in how I think, feel about myself, and act towards others, as well as in my ability to hear from God.

To think that we are unaffected by what we watch, read, or listen to is deceptive thinking. If you process anything like I do, you've probably thought to yourself, _I can handle this; it won't affect me._ But Paul had a reason for saying, "Have nothing to do with them."

Again, I can't stress enough how much I don't believe Scripture is saying to become self-righteous separatists. Paul is not saying to stop loving and reaching out. Instead, I believe he is saying that we must remove ourselves from being inundated with the lies, deceptions, and immorality that is often promoted—regardless of how funny, heartwarming, or interesting it can all be.

> **Look back at 2 Timothy 3:14-16.**
> **What does Paul tell us to continue in?**

The Holy Scriptures which is to make us wise.

According to verse 16, what is Scripture useful for?

Is profitable for reproof, for correction, for instruction in righteousness.

PERSONAL REFLECTION: Paul tells us to continue in what we've been convinced of in the Scriptures. Do you routinely read, listen to, or watch programs, movies, magazines, or music with messages that attempt to convince you otherwise?

Just in case you're getting nervous, this is not the part where I ask you to burn your CDs in a bonfire, throw your television out of a second-story building, or snip your cable wires (unless you want to). But it is the part where I hope you can be open to what God may want to purify in your life. You may have been wrestling with something as you've gone through today's study, wondering if it justifiably has a place in your life. Maybe it's one of those must-have indulgences that you want to justify but are ultimately not sure you can.

Without being legalistic, but simply being obedient, ask yourself: are you willing to let it go to pursue the truth? Write your thoughts below.

Scripture is "useful for teaching, rebuking, correcting and training in righteousness, so that the man of God may be thoroughly equipped for every good work" (2 Tim. 3:16). The wisdom of Scripture and the truth of God are ultimately to equip us for carrying out good in our lives. And I'm totally afraid we are routinely putting ourselves in front of things that compromise the good the Lord wants to accomplish in us. In a sense, we are allowing ourselves to be robbed.

> I'm totally afraid we are routinely putting ourselves in front of things that compromise the good the Lord wants to accomplish in us.

One of my dear friends in Florida recently told me she was convicted to give up a certain show. First of all, I have to address this word *convicted*. It's often used in the church in the context of someone saying they were convicted not to do something anymore. I normally encounter it being expressed in a sullen tone, like *I really wish this didn't happen, but the Lord convicted me that I shouldn't _____. Darn, I wish I hadn't heard that.* I used to hate being convicted. Sister, I know you've been there.

This is the case with my friend in Florida. She's really bummed out that she "can't" watch her show anymore and is—somewhat jokingly—looking for loopholes. I'm only using my friend as an example because we're close enough, I adore her, and I've all too often been in the same place. But what I'm realizing is that true conviction doesn't look for loopholes, and it isn't sad.

Of course, we may feel grief when parting with something we enjoy, but if true conviction is present, we will begin to look at that thing as something that was taking the place of God, something that was stealing from us. As we rid it from our lives we will be hopeful with anticipation, anxious to see what God will do in this newly-created space. We will not look for loopholes. We will be resolved. We will know that we are in a position to gain, not to be stolen from any longer.

Take these truths to heart if at any time today you have felt the Holy Spirit's conviction. It's a good thing. Go with it. Don't be sad and don't look for loopholes. Conviction is good; I've actually come to love it.

DAY 05 LIES
BEHIND EVERY FALSE GOD LURKS A PROWLING LION

We were at Lauri's the other night, eating homemade apple pie in her living room and discussing this whole issue of lies. By the way, I would recommend apple pie while discussing lies as it makes the whole experience so much more enjoyable. So does a little music. I had Alli take center couch with her guitar in Lauri's living room that night to sing a song she had written called "Liar's Dream."

If you have just a few minutes, grab the song off the Web site, light a candle, get in your favorite chair, and let the words and music become part of your own story. It's a great way to cap off the week.

LIAR'S DREAM [1]
ALL I WANT TO SAY IS THAT I'M SORRY
AND I DON'T EVEN KNOW WHY I'M ANGRY ANYMORE
THE ROAD JUST KEEPS ON GETTING LONGER
AND I'M GETTING OLDER AND I DON'T KNOW HOW
BUT I CAN'T RUN AWAY
TO PLACES WHERE THE WIND BLOWS

CHORUS:
I'VE HANDED OVER EVERYTHING I OWN
TO A LIAR'S DREAM
I'VE GIVEN IT MY VERY HEART AND SOUL
BUT THEY CAN'T SAVE ME NOW

I WISH IT WEREN'T SO HARD TO BE FORGIVING
I'M HURTING FROM THE PAIN
THAT DOESN'T LIVE HERE ANYMORE
AND IF I REALLY HAVE TO LEAVE IT ALL BEHIND
I WILL NOT KNOW HOW
BUT I CAN'T RUN AWAY
TO PLACES WHERE THE WIND BLOWS

I BELIEVE THERE'S A WAY
WHEN THINGS SEEM OUT OF CONTROL

CHORUS

1 Peter 5:8
Your enemy the devil prowls around like a roaring lion looking for someone to devour.

Post your comments on the discussion boards at: *http://www.lifeway.com/livingroomseries*

THE CYCLE IS TIRED OF REPEATING
AND I'VE GOT TO MOVE ON
'CAUSE I CAN'T KEEP RUNNING AWAY
TO PLACES WHERE THE WIND BLOWS
I'VE GOT TO BELIEVE THAT THERE'S A WAY
WHEN THINGS SEEM OUT OF CONTROL
LETTING GO IS NOT ROMANTIC

CHORUS
NO THEY CAN'T SAVE, MY HEART CAN'T SAVE ME NOW
JESUS SAVE ME NOW

I love Alli's song. It's the flesh and bones, and really blood, of what happens when we buy into a liar's dream. How brilliant of a title!

As we close the week out, I want us to be reminded of the ultimate false god who prowls behind all our lesser ones. It is Satan himself. I don't want us reading up on him for the sake of sparking fear in our hearts—we already know that our God reigns supreme over him. My hope is that we can be reminded of his tactics so we can more easily identify the lies he promotes.

Read each verse below and write in your own words their descriptions of Satan.

John 8:43-44 Murderer, no truth in Satan,
liar and father of lies.

2 Corinthians 11:14
Satan transformed himself to an angel of light

1 Peter 5:8
The devil walks around like a roaring lion
seeking whom he can devour.

Revelation 20:2
Satan will be bound for 1,000 years and cast into
the bottomless pit.

PERSONAL REFLECTION: How do these descriptions play into the lies you have believed?

Read Hebrews 6:18. Fill in the blank below.
It is impossible for God to lie or change his promises

Not only doesn't God lie; it's impossible for Him to do so!

I really take this for granted, but I'm so thankful I don't have to worry about God lying to me. Not only doesn't He lie; it's impossible for Him

72

to do so! When I juxtapose this truth against Satan, who is the father of lies, I am reminded of my need to vigilantly know God's truth while being able to identify the deceptions of the Enemy.

Before you close out with a written prayer, relax for a minute and take in a personal story from Carrie.

It was the day before Thanksgiving, and John and I were trying to pack our stuff before leaving for the long weekend. Naturally, the day was a bit more stressful than normal and my senses were somewhat heightened. I can't even remember what happened, except that John and I got into some sort of an argument that we never really discussed until later that day in the car. I remember getting angrier and more emotional as the minutes wore on. Somewhere in our discussion I realized that I had been imagining and acting out scenarios in my mind that hadn't actually happened, yet I proceeded as if they had.

In a moment it all clicked in my head that I CONSTANTLY believe LIES!!! I know this may sound obvious, but for so long—and even as we were sitting at Lauri's house talking about lies this week—I was thinking about the "big" lies that we believe: "You're not good enough," "So and so sings way better than you," "Nobody really likes you." These, to me, are the clear and obvious lies from Satan—but sometimes it's harder to discern the other constant, little lies that connect to the "big lies"—the ones that help accomplish the goal of us believing those big ones.

To give you a better idea of what this looks like—sometimes I find myself playing out a situation that's happened in real life and then start adding to it in my mind. Like what the person involved in the situation might have been thinking when they responded a certain way, or what their motives were behind their actions. Really, when it gets right down to it, I realize that most of the time they weren't thinking those things at all. I allow my emotions and actions to be dictated as a result of believing that what I dream up in my head has actually happened.

I have always known that one of Satan's major tactics is to deceive and lie to us. I guess I never realized that these "small" imaginations that capture my brain ARE the major LIES that I believe. I then allow those lies to negatively taint my attitude. My responses and treatment of others turn sour, emotional wellbeing is severely damaged, overall mental happiness is challenged, and on and on … you get the picture.

I think one of the reasons that this discovery has been so huge for me is because I have really been struggling with being unhappy about my overall attitude, whether it's an outward response or just an internal attitude. I feel like I now have a new weapon to battle the root of where this is coming from. I now can identify what's going on in my head and walk away from the lies—even though sometimes they're subtle.

So that's my little revelation…

End today by writing out a prayer in the margin for God's truth and an awareness of Satan's lies. Use words and language that are personal to you.

---

1. Written by Alli Rogers. Copyright Alli Rogers Music Inc. 2006.

CARRIE'S CHICKEN SCALLOPINI
SERVES 5

5 chicken breasts, butterflied
¾ c. milk
1 egg white
1 c. Italian bread crumbs
2 cloves fresh garlic
extra virgin olive oil
1 can (or more) chicken broth
1 can artichoke hearts
½ c. sun-dried tomatoes, chopped
1 lb. angel hair pasta

Butterfly chicken breasts. Cover each piece in a piece of plastic wrap (on both sides) and roll thin with rolling pin or mallet. Beat egg white in with milk. Put chicken breasts in the milk mixture. Dip each milk-covered chicken breast in bread crumbs and lightly cover. Put garlic and oil into large skillet. Oil should lightly cover entire pan. Let the garlic cook on medium to mix flavor in with the oil for 1 minute. Drop breaded chicken into skillet and cook on one side until crispy brown. Flip chicken and cook until light brown. Add more oil if needed. Add ½ cup chicken broth into side of skillet (careful not to dump it onto the top of crispy brown chicken). Add artichoke hearts and sun-dried tomatoes into skillet. Slowly add more chicken broth as you allow chicken to cook. Cover skillet to keep broth from cooking down too much. Boil water and cook pasta.

Strain pasta and cover with a little olive oil and set aside. Remove chicken breasts when they are finished cooking. Combine the pasta and the broth mixture from the skillet; then serve chicken over the pasta.

Note: If you want a thicker sauce, add some cornstarch to the broth and boil for a minute. Capers also add a great flavor to the mix.

THE PROBLEM WITH IDOLS
PEOPLE GODS

THE PROBLEM WITH IDOLS. REALLY.

WHERE DO YOU START? ISAIAH 44 MIGHT SAY IT BEST. THEY ARE A LIE. THEY DON'T DELIVER WHAT THEY PROMISE. THEY MISLEAD; THEY ADDICT; THEY DESTROY. AND, AGAIN, IF IT HASN'T BEEN EMPHASIZED ENOUGH OVER THE PAST FEW WEEKS, OUR FUNCTIONAL GODS DON'T NECESSARILY HAVE TO COME FROM THE INFAMOUS "BAD LIST" OF ALCOHOLISM AND SEXUAL OR DRUG ADDICTION. THEY CAN BE THE SIMPLE THINGS, EVEN THE GOOD THINGS, THAT ROB US IN THE END.

Ah, and yes, the worst gods of all can be people. They are easy gods, but never good ones. To be painfully honest, they have been my greatest seducer when it comes to idols. Perhaps this is why people who function as gods to us are the catalyst for pop-psychology words like codependent, unhealthy, and dysfunctional. People-gods end up very messy, and I say this for two reasons: first, because the Bible reveals this from cover to cover (how ancient its words but modern its principles), and second, because I have experienced the entangling and heartbreaking repercussions myself.

I just had dinner with a friend. She's a newbie to Nashville and a beautifully fresh complement to my life. We were discussing female friendships and their especially sacred place to us as women, but particularly as single women. We traded personal experiences of how each of us had become possessive of different people in our lives, be it boyfriends or female friends. I shared how miserable the results had been of placing people on pedestals—miserable for both them and me. Them, because they couldn't live up to my demands and expectations, and me, because they couldn't live up to my demands and expectations. Good times.

Because relationships are so necessary—as I believe God created them to be—the line can get awful fuzzy between codependent and healthy, deep friendships. This reminds me of an e-mail Anadara recently blasted to the nogs. I saved it for this exact moment:

Last night I was writing in a calendar-style "prayer journal" (can you say "New Year's Resolution"?) that I had from last year. Some of the dates have been filled in already, but I'm so sporadic about it that I

figured I'd save paper and just write in the same one this year. A year ago I was praying for God's comfort because I got stood up by TWO people who were supposed to meet me at the Station Inn ... I ended up spending the night there by myself and wrote in the journal when I came home because of course I felt so rejected.

Well, just yesterday morning I was replaying that whole scenario in my mind and thinking of reasons why they wouldn't have wanted to come see me etc. etc. etc.! I had formed all kinds of scenarios in my mind as to why I got stood up. I suddenly realized that these were lies Satan had been feeding me for A YEAR! Lame ones too. They turned out not even to be accurate reasons.

I came across a few other prayers asking God to give me victory in another difficult relationship I'm still dealing with, mostly because I'm insecure and afraid ... there go some more LIES! It was a great wake-up call that I needed to nip those lies in the bud so I could get on with my LIFE.

I appreciated Anadara's open struggle in this situation. She'd have needed to be brain dead not to hurt. Her feelings of rejection were normal and reasonable. What intrigued me most about her e-mail was her admirable admission to nursing her wound for an entire year, building her own story line on the initial hurt. I was intrigued because I have been so guilty of the same, and I'm sure to a much greater degree than she. (I have a vivid imagination, not usually to my benefit.) I was so proud of her for calling herself out on it, realizing that she had added lots of extra information to the injury. Who can't relate?

Relationships are difficult and can be devastating. But I've found that wrestling my pain out before God is the only healing salve for my brokenness. I believe the Lord has allowed me to go through some immensely painful relationships for the greater good of drawing me deeper into Him. I've gotten to know Him more richly in my losses. And I've learned to love people more deeply in the process. I am reminded of a verse in Philippians that I prayed several years ago and continue to pray: "I pray this: that your love will keep on growing in knowledge and every kind of discernment, so that you can determine what really matters and can be pure and blameless in the day of Christ" (Phil. 1:9-10, HCSB).

I had not really thought too much of wanting my love to abound in knowledge and discernment before the Lord brought this verse to my attention. The whole thing sounded a little clinical for my romantic musings until I realized how specifically this piece of God's Word spoke into my relationships.

Knowledge and discernment are necessary elements of our love as they allow us to understand what is best, what really matters. They leave no room for pettiness or exclusion. How often I've missed what REALLY MATTERED in a relationship. At times people became my own self-serving gods, causing me to lose track of what was important.

As I began praying this prayer my focus shifted over time. God Himself met my needs, which freed me up from looking for "life" from people. I was free to serve, pray, and give in my relationships. The inevitable hurt that comes with relational territory became exactly that—hurt—not devastating blows. I began to learn discernment rather than giving way to reckless imaginations of further hurt. This did not happen overnight and it is a progressive process for me, but one in which God has greatly grown me up.

As I sat with my friend the other night, I tried to describe the newfound freedom and perspective God has given me in relationships. Yes, I still get my feelings hurt, I sometimes desire exclusivity, I can feel left out, and I am tempted to possess and cling. But … and this is really a big "but," people-gods have lost their power. God is God in my life. He is Sovereign. Comforter. Friend. Guide. Light. He is personal, and nothing fills me more than His Presence and knowing that I am walking open handed in His will. Friendships—and how I hope one day a husband—are glorious complements to my life, which is quite different from them *being* my life. Quite different indeed.

DAY 01 THE PROBLEM WITH IDOLS
DESIRES GONE CRAZY

James 4:3
When you ask, you do not receive, because you ask with wrong motives, that you may spend what you get on your pleasures.

I'm wondering if certain thoughts have crossed your mind during the course of this study. They go something like … *What's the big deal? What's wrong with a few things I'm a little too dependent on? Everyone has excessive attachments to something.* I don't know if you've had these thoughts or not, but if you have, you're in familiar company. This issue of false gods can be deceiving. Of course everyone knows the big, bad ones are destructive, but it's often the subtler ones that cause just as much chaos.

I realize it can get tedious, this business of looking at functional gods, but I want to remind you of why we're here and where we're headed. The desired end is to make room for the one and only God. When our hearts are overly attached or dependent on lesser things, we crowd God out of our lives. It is impossible to serve God and gods.

What I'm getting at is this: I would be remiss if this journey became simply about ridding ourselves of idols because they're "bad" or because we want to be "good Christians." Far more is at stake. It's not just that they're wrong; it's that they're destructive. They steal from us. Lie to us. Harm us. It must be one of the reasons God gave us Exodus 20:1-6 (no other gods before Him), which we looked at our very first day.

The commandment is direct and straightforward. It really gives no reasons why we shouldn't serve other gods, except that God says not to. It reminds me of that universal thing moms say to their whining children all over the world, every day, in every tribe and tongue— *because I said so.* That really used to drive me nuts, but I suppose if I ever have children I will say the same thing, along with *eat the rest of your vegetables because there are kids starving in other countries …*

Though the Ten Commandments are just that—commandments, apart from any explanation as to why we should keep them—I would like to suggest that the rest of the Bible answers that question over and over again. The devastating fallout from idol worship, be it graven images, people, jewelry, planets, animals, the ability to bear children, or food, appears throughout Scripture. As I have studied the Bible over the years, I have found it very endearing that often God tells us what to do, and then shows us why. This week we'll look at both the show and tell elements of the destructive nature of idol worship—again, think functional gods, think modern-day idols, think personal stuff in your life.

Jumping right in ... let's look at some of the fallout issues that stem from idolatry—jealousy, bitterness, strife, anger, and even murder. We can always trace these issues back to threats to a functional god. James 4:1-5 gives some insight into why this is so.

> Read James 4:1-5. We're only going to look at a few verses today, so go especially slow, drinking in each concept. The passage is packed with profound ideas.

> What does James say causes struggles among us (v. 1)?

Struggles come from your desires for pleasure.

> Personalize the answer. What kind of desires battle within you (the ones that cause fights and unrest in your relationships with yourself and others)?

Look at the beginning of verse 2. The HCSB reads, "You desire and do not have. You murder and covet and cannot obtain." The word *desire* (or crave or lust) is taken from the Greek word *epithumio*, which literally means "to set the heart upon, i.e. long for (rightfully or otherwise)—covet, desire, lust (after)." This is key to more fully understanding what James is saying.

> Based on this definition, are the cravings that often cause us pain or get us into trouble necessarily desires for wrong or evil things? ☒ yes ☐ no

I heard Tim Keller, pastor of Redeemer Presbyterian Church in New York City, say, "Idolatry is attached to everything. All of our bitterness, all our impurity, all our malice, all of our problems, everything that troubles us is a result of idolatry. And what is idolatry? *It's taking a good thing and making it an ultimate thing*" (emphasis mine).

I fully agree with him, though I would also add that, of course, a bad thing can become an ultimate thing as well. However, in the sermon from which this quote is taken, Dr. Keller's thrust was simply this: We don't have to be craving evil things for an idol to be in the making; in fact, more often than not our desires are for perfectly good things, as we've discussed earlier. I believe this is exactly what James is saying. He's explaining that our *epithumio* (our desires for even good things) often cause heartache and devastation when they are excessive or inordinate.

I wonder if this definition changes the way you would answer that question about the desires that battle in you. I've read the book of James many times, conjuring up all the desires I had for "bad" and "evil" things, convinced that those were the problem. It never occurred to me that my desires for perfectly good things could turn excessive and disproportionate, causing all the great pain and unrest that James describes.

Speaking of these things, look again at James 4:1-2 and write below the detrimental things that result from our *epithumio*.

Lust, murder, covet, fight, war

This list is succinct but horrific: fights, wars, murders, and covetousness. Again, isn't it surprising that these things come as a result of inordinate, excessive affections for things that oftentimes are inherently good?

One of the struggles that immediately comes to my mind is the struggle for relationship. Though I don't want to pigeonhole the female nature on any level, I think that the pervasive desire to be loved and chosen is especially innate in us. This is a very good thing. I believe it's a God-given thing. However, we've all been on both sides of what happens when this desire becomes the dominating force in a person's life. I've seen friendships and marriages utterly destroyed over an obsessive and consuming desire to be loved by someone.

I have a college friend who got married right after graduation. Elated is the only word I can think of to describe her. She had captured the heart of "wonder boy," and everyone was thrilled but a little jealous at the same time. He was exceptionally attractive, athletic, smart, and

82

spiritual. The two of them went on to have beautiful children, and I remember thinking how perfectly my friend had it. A few months ago I was shocked to hear of their impending divorce. I couldn't believe it.

Though things like divorce are always more complicated than just one issue, it turns out that my friend's insecurity and her desperate desire to be loved in a way that no human can ever provide was the major catalyst behind her crumbling marriage. She kept abnormal tabs on her husband, questioned him relentlessly, and obsessively tried to control his every move.

When I think of my friend alongside our passage in James, I see a good desire gone wrong. Yes, it was good and wonderful that she desired to be loved by her husband; but when that desire became obsessive and over-the-top, it caused fights, marital wars, and ultimately divorce. At the very root, her husband had become her idol, her god, her savior. And no matter how amazing a person is, humans always make terrible gods.

> **Look again at verses 3-5. What does James call the people who are "friends of the world"?** *Adulterers Paduteresses* **(Note that his reference to the world is referring to the world system, the things that are contrary to God, His truth, and His love.)**

I used to view this passage as frightful and severe. I'd rather avoid being called an adulteress in my morning quiet time. And yet—without watering anything down   if I look at it in the appropriate light, I can see the warning as affectionately loving.

I look at it this way: the only way people can be adulterous is if they're married. James in essence said, "Remember, you're married to Christ!" This is what the Apostle Paul taught when he referred to us as the bride of Christ. We are in union with Him. He is our provider, the lover of our souls, and our actual life. When we esteem the world, its beliefs, or anything in the world and make it our god (think of my friend's husband), it is as if we are breaking union with Christ, looking for our desires to be met elsewhere. In essence, all believers are married to Christ, so when we look to idols we are being unfaithful to Him. This idolatry is the root of jealousy, which is the root of fighting and quarrels and wars.

The encouraging news is that James presents a way out of this cyclical agony. We'll be spending a lot more time at the end of the week seeing how; but for now, slowly read verses 6-10 in James 4.

> **Fill in the blank. In verse 8, James asks us to draw near to God. He tells those who are sinning to cleanse their hands and those who are double- _minded_ to purify themselves.**

I think it's a perfectly fitting label for our topic of false gods. When God told us to have no other gods before Him, it was built-in protection from being double-minded. If we are serving God and God alone, we are single-minded with one focus. When we claim God is our God while we are serving false gods, we become double-minded and unstable.

> **In closing, write about an area of your life where you have been double-minded. After you've finished writing, think and pray about what needs to happen to be single-minded again. Then, as James so eloquently writes, "Draw near to God."**

DAY 02 THE PROBLEM WITH IDOLS
JEALOUSY AND COMPETITION

Yesterday James told us what happens when our desires rule and the object of our desires becomes a false god. The next few days we'll look at the story of Leah and Rachel as an example. I learn by seeing and touching the real-life stories of women who have struggled with the same things I have.

There's more reading than normal today, but it's story reading, which is easier I think. Enjoy the drama. Be encouraged that we modern-day women did not invent the lovely outcroppings of jealousy and strife.

> Read Genesis 29:16-30 to get some background. A quick read will do it. Afterward, answer the questions below.

> Who did Jacob desire to marry? ❑ Leah   ☑ Rachel   ❑ both

> How did Laban deceive Jacob?
> ❑ Giving him Rachel first but doubling the amount of time he had to work for her.
> ❑ Giving him Leah and giving Rachel to Esau.
> ☑ Giving him Leah first and then Rachel after making him agree to another seven years of work.
> ❑ Making him work 14 years and giving him no one.

Laban deceived Jacob and gave him Leah as his wife even though he knew he wanted to marry Rachel. After Jacob protested, Laban agreed to give Rachel to him as well, but also made him agree to another seven years of work.

Now that we have the backstory, let's look at the heart of what I hope will bless you as much as it has me. Though it's honestly a sad and depressing story, I think there are principles here that—if we grasp hold of them—can make our lives dramatically different.

> Read Genesis 29:31–30:24. Take mental note of the names that Leah gives her children and what they mean.

> Genesis 29:31 very plainly states that Leah was not _loved_.

Hosea 2:19
I will betroth you to me forever; I will betroth you in righteousness and justice, in love and compassion.

PERSONAL REFLECTION: Describe the last time you felt unloved by someone you wanted to love you.

Some of us might have to go back to junior high to remember being rejected by someone who didn't love us. Others might be in the middle of a marriage or a deep relationship where they are unloved or at least feel unloved. Some have grown up with a parent or parents who didn't love them. Though I can't imagine the depths of what you might have gone through or are currently experiencing, I know God sees. He saw Hagar and Hannah, and here He saw Leah. Not as a replacement for love, but as a blessing, God gave Leah children. Instead of seeing the gift of children as an end in itself, however, Leah viewed her children as a way to capture the heart of her husband.

Though all the names of Leah's children are important, I want to focus in on a few that have to do with what we're studying. Next to each name listed below, fill in Leah's hope that accompanied each name.

1. **Reuben (29:32)** Lord heard Leah was unloved He gave her a son,

2. **Levi (29:34)** Husband has become attached to her

3. **Zebulun (30:20)** Now husband will dwell with me.

This is where I really relate to Leah. Out of my own desperate desire to be chosen and loved, I have often hoped that what I could bring to the table would win the heart of the person I wanted to love me. For Leah, having children was a way of trying to garner love, honor, and acceptance from Jacob. For me, it was trying to look better, be better, achieve more, offer my time and resources—anything that might attract attention. The major hitch for Leah in all her childbearing was that Jacob's heart was solely for Rachel. No amount of children was going to change the fact that he didn't really love her.

I want to go just a little further into this painful story, but hopefully for an ending that's ultimately encouraging. Did you notice how increasingly desperate Leah got for any amount of affection or presence she could get from Jacob? Look at the progression. With

Reuben, she was hoping for love; with Levi, she was hoping for attachment; with Zebulun, she was just hoping to be treated with respect.

> **Also, go back to verses 30:14-16. Ponder Leah's desperation and write how this translates in your own life. (For example, when have you—or are you now—acting out of this kind of desperation?)**

Did you notice that Leah didn't even wait for Jacob to get home? Instead, she went out to meet him in the field in order to tell him that he was sleeping with her that night. Let these thoughts sink in: she knew she wasn't loved, she knew she had given him everything she had and it wasn't enough, and she knew that Rachel would always be chosen. And still … she ran out to meet him for just one night of something that might feel just a little like love.

> **PERSONAL REFLECTION: Write about a time where you were willing to give yourself to someone for merely crumbs in return. It doesn't have to be sexual in nature or involve the opposite sex. It could be a friend, child, parent, or boss as well.**

We've read a lot today. Let the story permeate your heart. Let Leah's predicament mingle into your own longings and desperations for true love—the ones we've all had if we're honest. Also, ask the Holy Spirit to reveal the vacuum of desperation that may reside inside you. There's Someone more sustaining and more fit to fill it than even the best of our Jacobs.

> **If this story feels painfully close to home, meditate on Psalm 146 in closing. There is hope and refreshment for your soul.**

There's Someone more sustaining and more fit to fill our hearts than even the best of our Jacobs.

DAY 03 THE PROBLEM WITH IDOLS
MORE JEALOUSY AND COMPETITION

Proverbs 27:20, KJV
So the eyes of man are
never satisfied.

Yesterday we focused exclusively on Leah, but today we're going to look at the other woman in the account, Rachel. Before we go any further, I'm assuming that yesterday you picked up on the moral of the story: those who are beautiful and desired by men are happy, and those who are homely and unloved are miserable. Sounds conventional enough. Seems reasonable. Certainly agrees with our culture and media. Oh. Except that as I recall, Rachel was miserable too.

This was confusing to me. Rachel had everything Leah wanted and was convinced would make her happy: she had the exclusive love of Jacob, not to mention she was physically stunning. But you're probably remembering from yesterday that she couldn't have children and perhaps you would argue—like me—that was the reason why she was so miserable. If only that could be taken care of, she'd be complete and satisfied. Let's see if this theory is correct …

> **Reread Genesis 30:1-3. Why did Rachel want to die?**
>
> *She wanted children*

> **Of whom was Rachel jealous (v. 1)?**
>
> *Leah*

After all the lamenting, heartbreak, and misery Leah had lived through she was still the object of someone's jealousy. Look at verse 3 and notice the desperation that Rachel showed by settling for a child through her maidservant. Don't you think Rachel's attitude was similar to the desperate nature of Leah when she was willing to settle for a night with Jacob? Both women were hanging on to mere threads; both were willing to hold out for crumbs. It is the saddest picture, yet one that so many of us live out on a regular basis.

So many women are so desperate for love that they'll do just about anything to get whatever feels mildly close. We've all known women who were willing to have sex for a night just to be held, just to feel like someone desired them, even for a moment. Or maybe you don't just know that woman, but you are that woman. Without inflicting any shame, I write to you passionately: there is a better way! But we'll save that for the end.

I want to stay with Rachel just a bit longer to see what happens when she finally gets the desire of her heart. In Genesis 30:23, you'll remember that Rachel gave birth to her first son, Joseph. Fill in the rest of the phrase: "God has taken away my _reproach_ " (NIV).

Leah was not loved. Rachel was disgraced. Both believed that their answer lay with someone other than God. For Leah, it was the love of Jacob. For Rachel, it was having children. The difference between the two was that Rachel finally got everything she had wanted. God opened her womb, and she gave birth to Joseph.

Rachel had the exclusive love of her husband, and now she had the firstborn son she had always wanted. So in my mind I'm thinking she should finally be happy. She should be satisfied, filled, contented, at rest. Though we don't get a lot more details about the rest of her life, this next passage I find to be somewhat telling.

Turn slightly ahead and read Genesis 31:32-35. What did Rachel steal? Laban's idols

So my theory is not holding up well. Apparently being beautiful, loved, and physically fruitful is not enough. Apparently the son that Rachel always longed for didn't quite fill the void in her life. Somehow her striking beauty and the focused love of her husband didn't do it. She had it all, and yet she still needed false gods. This is so profound to me.

PERSONAL REFLECTION:

1. Describe a time when you finally got the very thing/person you had longed for and it didn't make you as happy as you thought it would.

2. Write about something/someone you don't have but are convinced would make you happy if you could obtain it.

Before we go further, I want to be careful not to sound harshly critical of Leah and Rachel. I actually identify with them on several levels—probably mostly with Leah. I don't sit in judgment of their behavior. I feel for their plight, wishing that both of them could have found in God the rest their souls so desperately needed. I can't say enough about the irony of their story. In fact, I was really hoping that the New Testament referenced them so I could get a little more insight. The sad story of both Rachel and Leah ends abruptly, and there's hardly another word written about them.

Just a few weeks ago I was asking God what the point (or moral) of this depressing account was. Leah was homely and unloved and seemingly miserable. Rachel was beautiful and loved and finally got children, yet she was cramming idols into her bag on the way out. God, what's the point here? What's the takeaway? I didn't get it.

By no means do I feel like the final authority on this passage, yet I felt the Lord answer my question in a surprising way. It's as if He said, *That is the point!* It's so much simpler than I had been making it. The point is that it doesn't matter if you have it all and get everything your heart desires, or if you're left wanting and unloved. Neither works. The two women had vastly different circumstances, yet both were left hungry. Why? Because God was not their ultimate thing. Good things like husbands and children and social status were the ultimate things, and in the end they were not enough. In fact, so much so for Rachel that she was found grasping for gods near the end of her life.

And all of this leads me back to my statement earlier that a better way exists. I do not say this tritely, because I've experienced God's satisfying nature after many rounds with lesser things. I've experienced it after the pain of laying down the things in which I had originally put my hope.

I believe obedience is the precursor to experiencing God's satisfying presence and the richness of His blessings. This is not a formula but a path that manifests itself in a relationship that is honest and open between God and us. It functions supremely when we are looking solely to Him as Savior.

I want to end with a personal note to those of us who see pieces or entire chunks of ourselves in Rachel and Leah. To those who grasp for threads and hold out for crumbs. To those whose desperation for

I believe obedience is the precursor to experiencing God's satisfying presence and the richness of His blessings.

love and affection has led us down unimaginably devastating roads. To those who have found it and realize it's not enough. To those who believe if we could just have … we would finally be happy.

I am you. I have been there. I have found myself in both the shoes of Leah and Rachel: Leah's when I am miserable because I lack, and Rachel's when I am miserable in my fullness. The way out? Jesus Christ.

Part of me hesitates to write something so simple. Yet when you encounter Him and begin to take Him at His words through obedience, His name doesn't mean easy answers but power and love and life-sustaining freedom.

God has created each of us uniquely and specifically. He knows the longings of our hearts. He sees our pain. He hears our cries. The element of obedience is simply a way of life that agrees with God. It is the only way for us to truly experience the satisfying life and love of God. He will do the rest. Your life does not need to end up like either of these women. In fact, John 10:10, in essence, says that Jesus Christ has come so that you no longer have to grasp and strain at mere hints of what your heart desires. He has come "that [you] may have life, and have it to the full." We'll be looking at this in greater depth tomorrow and the next day. There's hope ahead.

God has created each of us uniquely and specifically. He knows the longings of our hearts.

DAY 04 THE PROBLEM WITH IDOLS
THEY CAN'T SATISFY

Ephesians 2:4-5
Because of his great love for us, God, who is rich in mercy, made us alive with Christ.

The story of Rachel and Leah is so dense with implications for us that it's almost frustrating. I find myself constantly wanting to interject, *and another thing* … Sometimes it's hard to know what to highlight, which is why I'm so thankful that 1 John 2:27 says that the Holy Spirit teaches us individually.

I'm sure as you've been reading the Lord has touched you with things that I've never thought of and haven't mentioned anywhere in this study. Hold fast to those things—they're the most important.

Since the theme this week is the problem of idols, I want to summarize a few things. We began the week looking at James. We saw that an excessive desire, even for good things, can turn into idol worship. Idol worship produces the fallout of fighting, greed, anger, bitterness, and even murder.

We moved from James' letter to a very palpable story of two women who displayed some of the behavior James described because they felt their own idols being threatened. Though their lives were far from useless (Leah's son Judah is in the line of Christ, and Rachel bore Joseph), both seemed to exist fairly miserably.

Though you've already read these verses, go back to Genesis 30 and reread verses 1-15. This time specifically look for the "fallout" and list as many things as you see to be a result of their excessive desires and attachments.

Rachel blames Jacob, he gets angry.
Rachel gives Jacob- Bilhah her maid, who has two sons
Leah give Jacob- Zilpah her maid, who has 2 sons

I want to highlight jealousy as a significant result of false gods since it's so prevalent. I don't know how it is for you, but I'm not sure I hate any feeling more than when I'm overcome with jealousy. First off, the physical feeling that manifests itself in my stomach and body is

92

horrible. And second, I usually feel trapped in it, like the only thing I can do to make it go away is to go punch someone in the eye. That, or dissolve into a pile of tears. I've also noticed that an element of panic seems to be attached to my jealousy, as if I have to remedy the situation that moment by whatever means. I fully believe this is why we see people do unthinkable things in moments of jealous rage.

> **This streak of panic really shows up in Rachel after Leah gives birth to her fourth child. What phrase in Genesis 30:1 shows the panic element in her jealousy?**
>
> *Envy*
>
> **As Rachel's jealousy billowed it set off an extremely unreasonable request for Jacob—*give me children* (as if he totally controls that), *or else I'll die.* In verse 2, how does her out-of-control behavior cause Jacob to respond?**
>
> *angry*
>
> **What is Rachel's solution (v. 3)?** *maid Bilhah*

We've already discussed that jealousy feels terrible and is often accompanied by false urgency. Verse 3 reveals something additional it does—something we've all experienced at one point or another: it propels us to foolishly and inadequately attempt to remedy our situation (for example, Rachel giving her maidservant to Jacob to bear her child).

For Rachel, the idol of having children was so strong that it functioned as her life. Without them, she didn't want to live, so she had to do whatever it took to get children. They had become the "ultimate" thing, and people will do far crazier things when something threatens their ultimate thing.

Now that we've recapped the bad news, I'm assuming you're anxious to get to the brighter part of our study, the part that has to do with living above things like jealousy, bitterness, and anger. God has delivered me from so much of this entanglement—if not, I couldn't write this in good conscience. But more important than my experiences are God's words through Scripture, which, when applied, will be your own path of healing and transformation. You will wear His truths uniquely, and your story will be your own.

God's words through Scripture, when applied, will be your own path of healing and transformation.

Meditate on Ephesians 2:1-10. Look for any "keys" (forgive me for sounding so formulaic) to freedom from the consequences of idolatry. List your findings below.

We are made alive with Christ, and raised us up together, and made us to sit together in the heavenly places in Christ Jesus.

In closing today, look specifically at this portion of verse 3: "gratifying the cravings of our sinful nature and following its desires and thoughts." This is who we were before our old nature was put to death with Christ. When we trusted Him for forgiveness, heaven, and a relationship with Him, we were given a new life.

We no longer need to be controlled by our cravings and lusts. We are no longer bound to jealousy and revenge and bitterness when something is taken from us, when we are mistreated, or when we experience loss. Why? Because Jesus Christ shows the incomparable riches of His grace to us along with His kindness (v. 7). He becomes our ultimate thing, and the far lesser things that are threatened or compromised are nothing to be compared to who He is and what He can do for us.

When I used to read passages like Ephesians 2—and still to some degree—it seemed a little far off. How am I to put to death certain things, and what are the incomparable riches of Jesus? Simply believing the truth of my new life is an essential place to start. If you have trusted Christ, these things are true of you.

End today in a prayer of belief over Ephesians 2:1-10 (always knowing that you can ask God to help your unbelief). In prayer, read aloud what is true of you and believe the truth of it wherever you are.

DAY 05 THE PROBLEM WITH IDOLS
AND A FEW SOLUTIONS

After a week of studying and writing about some heavy and painful issues, last night I found myself wanting to air out with some simple Scripture meditation. I wanted to be reminded of who I am in Christ. To be refreshed by the truth that I am dearly loved by God and that He will provide love for me here on earth. His provision is so unique.

I also wanted to be reminded that because of Jesus' death and resurrection I am no longer bound to my earthly cravings that cause me so much heartache. I needed the knowledge that I can live in kindness, gentleness, forgiveness, and patience—that I don't need to resort to punching someone's lights out when they threaten the objects of my desires. Though we are constantly being transformed into the image of Christ and this process takes time, we have to begin by standing on the truth. We are *in* Christ and delivered from our old selves.

Today will be simple but profound. We haven't done this before, but I'm asking that you do what I did last night. Read Colossians 3:1-17 three times through. The multiple readings will cause certain things to surface that you might otherwise miss. You might want to try reading three different translations for further insight. As you read, be thinking in terms of everything we've studied this week. Corresponding with the numbers below, write what strikes you with each reading.

1. Set your mind on things above

2. I will appear in glory with Christ.

3. Put on kindness, humility

As verse 15 says, today "let the peace of God rule in your hearts."

**Colossians 3:16
Let the word of Christ dwell in you richly.**

EASY BEEF POT ROAST

This recipe can be adjusted according to how many people you are serving, the size of your slow cooker, and your personal preferences.

1-2 lbs. of any kind of beef roast
½ of an onion, sliced
1 bag baby carrots or 2 c. sliced carrots
6-7 red potatoes, halved
1-2 T beef base (see note)

Cut up veggies. Add an inch or two of warm water to a slow cooker and then stir in the beef base, a tablespoon for every pound of beef. Add the roast into the water; do not cut off the fat because it adds flavor. Add the onions on top of the meat, and then add the veggies. Only the meat should be covered by the water when you first turn on the cooker. Allow at least 8 hours to cook on low heat for best results. You can do it in less time by cooking on high heat for a few hours and then switching to low. Try not to open the lid after you start the cooking.

Note: Beef base can be found in most grocery stores near the bouillon in the soup aisle.

PUMPKIN MUFFINS
PREHEAT OVEN TO 350° MAKES 24 MUFFINS

2 c. sugar
1 c. vegetable or canola oil
4 eggs
2 c. pumpkin (not pumpkin pie filling)
2 c. flour
2 tsp. baking powder
1 tsp. cinnamon
⅛ tsp. ground cloves
⅛ tsp. nutmeg
1 tsp. baking soda
1 tsp. vanilla

Mix ingredients together in a large bowl. Put into muffin tins (sprayed with cooking spray) and bake 20-25 minutes. These are a great addition to a fall meal!

GOOD GOODBYES
SAYING GOODBYE

FOR THE MOST PART, IT SEEMS THAT GOODBYES HAVE A FAIRLY NEGATIVE CONNOTATION. HALF THE TIME I JUST AVOID THEM ALTOGETHER, EVEN IF LEAVING IS IMMINENT. LAST WEEK I WAS UP IN NORTHERN VIRGINIA, WHERE I GREW UP, FOR BUSINESS. I GOT TO FORGO THE SQUARE HOTEL ROOM FOR THE COMFORT AND AMENITIES OF HOME. AFTER WORKING ALL DAY I WAS HAPPY TO RETURN TO A HOUSE FULL OF FAMILY AND TOGETHERNESS, INSTEAD OF A QUIET HOTEL THAT SMELLED LIKE CLEANING SPRAY ATTEMPTING TO MASK CIGARETTE SMOKE. I SAVORED EACH INHALATION.

Mom whipped up dinners from scratch the way she's been doing my whole life. Although this time she was less like mom and more like sous-chef, overly accommodating our selective palettes. I was dying for her homemade pizza, while my pregnant sister Katie, whose appetite is currently odd and limited, wanted sweet potatoes with marshmallows. She claimed it was the only thing that wouldn't make her vomit all over the living room. My dad was happy to have the salmon my mom originally had on the menu, while my grandparents, who now live with my parents, had a hankering for fried chicken because they don't like sal-mon (they pronounce the "L").

I think my mom had about nine dinners going at the same time. After she pulled everything out of the oven and off the stove, we staked out our seats around the table—brother-in-law, pregnant sister, non-pregnant sister, brother's girlfriend, brother, mom, dad, grandparents, and me. Oddly enough, broccoli with melted cheese, sal-mon, sweet potatoes, hot rolls, fried chicken, *and* pizza all work well on the same plate.

After dinner we sat around playing a silly card game, which requires absolutely no strategy—I usually only bring this up when I'm losing though. My grandparents are ridiculous card sharks. I have to keep an eye on my Pop because he has no conviction about cheating. And I have no control over my Bammom (the unflattering name I gave her as a kid) because she plays within the rules but rarely within the lines of strategy. Her favorite card in this particular game is the "skip" card.

You can use it whenever and on whomever you want, although the average player will usually throw it against the player who's winning. Bammom does not adhere to this logic. Her discards are like aimless grenades. I think my mom was losing by about 100 points when she got up to fix Bammom some tea. As she was stirring in the honey, she heard from across the room, "Skip your mom!" This did not go over well. I suggested Mom just make her sal-mon for the rest of the week.

After cards we retired to the living room, where it seems like Jeopardy is always showing. It's a running nightmare of unanswerable, meaningless questions for me, which is why I peruse a magazine or something so as to look like I'm not paying attention (but in case I hear a question I might actually know, I can still answer and sound intelligent). My brother-in-law excels at this game, and my mom is right there with him. She'll clean your clock on anything that has to do with royalty. I always just guess Elizabeth the something or other. Occasionally this works out for me.

My dad is a genius in many areas I would never trade for trivia, but I wouldn't say this particular game is his strong suit. Years ago, when my brother David was a little boy, he would sit on my dad's lap every night for Jeopardy. One night he perked up, "Dad, I think you should go on the show." My dad's ego was aptly boosted. Proud that his son thought so highly of his intellect, he asked, "Why do you think I should be on Jeopardy?" David brilliantly explained, "Because the loser gets a free Nintendo." We love David for this line.

Having a full house is a delight to my personality, even when Jeopardy's on. Although I love my calm and controlled, one-bedroom, 500 square foot condo, it stands in sharp contrast to my parent's lively home in Virginia. It reminds me that I am not alone in the world, that I'm tied to people by blood and love, and that the struggles I think are unique to me, are not. The commotion of several generations piled on top of one another is hard, beautiful, exhilarating, and comforting. I can seamlessly go from untangling Pop's oxygen cord from around Bammom's cane to anxiously viewing the sonogram pictures of my niece-to-be. Why would I want to say goodbye to this?

Which is why I usually don't.

My flights are often early, meaning I can sneak out of the house before anyone is up. I'm always secretly happy about this, because it means I can avoid that fateful word, goodbye. No sad hugs. No I'll see you soon. I prefer creeping out the door without ever having to address the leaving. But of course—and you knew there was an "of course" coming—there are some goodbyes that are good, healthy, and to be celebrated. Perhaps still painful, but right nonetheless.

I'm not sure anything has ever been harder for me—the utterance of goodbyes, the playing out of them, their finality, their void, their distance. Yet there are some distances, some chasms, some signing offs that are purely necessary for life to blossom. Certain things—and I won't name them, because you already know them in your soul—choke us, wound us, and bind us in ways that keep us from new hellos. They deserve a farewell. Still we cling because the painful familiar is often more comfortable than the foreign amazing.

Until that foreign amazing grows into the beautiful familiar, and we think back to our old days of entangling gods and wonder why we didn't wave goodbye earlier. Yes, there's that awful parting, and there might even be an intermittent void; but how God fills the space when we make room for Him. How our good goodbyes can turn into unimaginably sweet and surprising hellos. The parting can feel terribly risky and lonely, but goodbyes aren't so bad when new hellos can be faintly heard around the corner. Practice your wave …

DAY 01 GOOD GOODBYES
FALSE MEMORIES

Deuteronomy 8:16
He gave you manna
to eat in the desert,
something your
fathers had never
known, to humble
and to test you so
that in the end it
might go well
with you.

Over the past few weeks we've looked at general and personal false gods. I happen to prefer studying the general ones; it's not nearly as invasive as looking at the ones that exist in my daily life. But if I only stuck with studying broad definitions of false gods, I would probably become a professional finger-pointer, which, incidentally, I've found people really don't like. Plus, I hope we can attain the freedom that comes by dealing head-on with the functional gods in our personal lives. So far, we've been naming them, defining them, praying against them. This week we'll be looking at leaving them. I'm not especially fond of goodbyes, but I've found that some are the only path to new hellos.

> **Read Numbers 11:1-17**
> **The Israelites who had been miraculously freed from Egypt aren't looking so good here. They had two major complaints.**
>
> **Fill in the blanks:**
> **They were sick of eating** manna .
> **They were craving** meat .

I guess the Israelites' desire sounds reasonable enough, especially by today's standards … the high-carb diet wasn't working for them. I, for one, would have been deliriously happy. To eat bread all day and have it be God-ordained—please, could there be anything better?

> **Okay, so it might not have been exactly what I have in mind. Exodus 16:31 says that the manna was like coriander seed, was white, and tasted like wafers made with honey. That still sounds pretty great to me, but look at Deuteronomy 8:3 and 8:16. According to these verses, what makes you think that manna might have been a no-frills type of food?**

Though God was using the manna to humble and test them, I love the positive promise at the end of verse 16, "to do thee good at thy latter end" (KJV), or "in the end it might go well with you" (NIV). Going through times of vast desert spaces and living on less than the bare minimum are not my favorite seasons. I say it was less than the bare minimum because the Lord said He didn't want them to live by bread alone.

The manna was not quite enough; it didn't fully suffice them. The Lord put them in this position so they would depend on Him and not on themselves, their provisions, or false gods. Not to mention, He wanted to do them good in the end. This is the "making room" piece. God wants to do us good! Too often we associate the idea of turning from our false gods with misery and legalism when really it means making room for God to do good in our lives.

Recently I was lamenting with a friend about my career. I told her how tired I was of struggling so hard for a living. I quickly amended my statement to "actually a little less than a living." She laughed at my qualification. She happens to write hit country songs for a living, so she can afford to laugh.

At any rate, I stopped to think about it further and realized that I really do make slightly less than a living, yet somehow I am totally provided for—and not in a woe-is-me kind of way either. Whatever I lack in what I can provide for myself, God fills with a sweet measure of provision unique to me and my values. The last several years you could say I've lived on manna, because I haven't been able to live on it alone. I have had to depend on God. In my best moments, that is.

God uses scarcity in our lives (it can be in any area, not just financial) to draw us to dependency on Himself. But we'll see He doesn't force us into this intimacy. Instead of relying on the Lord, the Israelites demanded meat from Him.

> **What word in Numbers 11:4 (NIV) is used to describe their desire for meat?**
> ❑ wanted ☒ craved ❑ needed ❑ hoped for

Needing and wanting are one thing. But craving (or lusting) implies something a bit more out of control—something ruling them. Citing an earlier definition, false gods can be good things. They become a problem when they control us or when we demand them. After all, having fish and cucumbers—and, I guess, leeks—are fine in and of themselves.

> **Think of an idol in your life that falls into this category of good. How is craving it different than wanting or needing it?**

Too often we associate the idea of turning from our false gods with misery and legalism when really it means making room for God to do good in our lives.

Looking back at Numbers 11:5, list the things they were remembering about Egypt.

Fish, cucumbers, melons, leeks, onions, and garlic

This next part not only fascinates me but also opens a psychological window into my own life and how I tend to remember my own times of entangled living. According to their memories, how much did they have to pay for all this (v. 5)?

Hang onto the phrase *at no cost* as you read Exodus 1:11-15; 2:23-25.

This is a rhetorical question, so you can rest your pens. Where in the world did "at no cost" come from? The Israelites were slaves in Egypt for 470 years. The Egyptians killed their baby boys. They were forced into hard labor, their taskmasters doubled their workload, and they were groaning before God. Were the fish, the melons, the onions, and the garlic really "at no cost"?

I remember a time when God was moving me on from something that was holding me captive. To stay away from too much rhetoric, I use the word *captive* in the sense that this particular thing seemed to control my behavior. I was struggling with balance in my life. As Tim Keller said, it was a good thing that had become an ultimate thing.

Many months after walking away from the situation, I began to remember the whole ordeal through rose-colored lenses. I had conveniently forgotten all the pain and angst that was associated with that time in my life. I was only remembering the "leeks" from that season. I had forgotten the disproportionate price I paid for them. I was remembering them at no cost when really they had cost me considerable parts of my life.

Perhaps you have said goodbye to some idols in your life but are currently missing them due to false memories of the time. Pray that God would give you clarity as you look back at what really took place during that time span. Write about it here—writing will help with clarity.

DAY 02 GOOD GOODBYES
OVERLY FULL

The whole idea of looking back at bad times in our life as somehow good and appealing was a dramatic discovery for me. It freed me from undue grief and sadness over things that didn't need to be mourned—if for no other reason than because those times really weren't that great. Ultimately I became glad I had left those things behind.

But I haven't always said goodbye to the things I should have. Or, just as often, I have said goodbye externally while my heart remained attached. I think this is where the Israelites were. They were somewhere between Egypt and the promised land, between full-on captivity and full-on freedom and blessing. Welcome to perils of the desert. Today we'll look at their demands on God and the consequences of their unwillingness to say goodbye.

> **Picking up where we left off yesterday, read Numbers 11:18-35.**
>
> **Your Take: Why do you think the Lord chose to give them what they craved?**
>
> *The people craved meat and cryed for it.*
>
> **PERSONAL REFLECTION: Has the Lord ever given you something you kept demanding, even though it wasn't a good thing? If so, explain.**

It's odd for me to think of God actually fulfilling our appetite for sin. And yet as soon as I write that, I'm realizing that He doesn't really fulfill it—He over-fills it. Which does exactly the opposite. It causes us to lose our appetite due to sickness and nausea as we overeat on what we were craving. We see that God gave them more than enough—so much more that meat was coming out of their nostrils and they were loathing it. Mmmmmmm. That's such a nice picture.

> **Psalm 106 gives us another writer's perspective on what happened when the people demanded meat from God in the desert. Read verses 7-15.**

Psalm 106:15, KJV
He gave them their request; but sent leanness into their soul.

I believe the Israelites' craving for meat was intensified not only by their glorified memories of Egypt but also by their forgetfulness of the good things God had done for them. What were some of the things they had forgotten about according to Psalm 106?

God rebuked the Red Sea and it dried up, and saved them from Pharoah and and they forgot all that

Isn't it interesting that they remembered how good the garlic was but failed to remember the Red Sea drying up? That coming-out-of-Egypt thing was great, but apparently it didn't hold a candle to those leeks.

Look specifically at verse 15. It says He gave them what they asked for, but *sent leanness into their souls*.

The KJV says, "He gave them their request; but sent leanness into their soul." I wonder if that's where they felt the real loss—in their souls.

Look up the word *lean* or *leanness* in the dictionary (in this context, not to lean against something) and write its definition below.
Lean (leanness):

God's judgment is filled with irony. He gave them so much that they were left with very little. Physically they were fat, but their souls were anemic.

Describe a time when you finally got what you wanted, but it left you lean in soul.

We deceive ourselves when we think our gods will bring us anything but leanness of soul.

Today feels like such a foundational study to me. We deceive ourselves when we think our gods will bring us anything but leanness of soul. In the Israelites' case, they were offered the minimalist diet of manna so that their souls could feast on the Lord (remember, He didn't want them to live by bread alone). Instead, they craved the richness of quail while their souls starved.

You could say that God wanted bread for their bodies so they could have meat for their souls; instead they demanded meat for their bodies but got bread for their souls.

In light of all this, do whatever you feel led to do today. Meditate further, pray, write, take a walk—whatever will feed your soul.

DAY 03 GOOD GOODBYES
COURAGE FOR CHANGE

During the aftermath of Hurricane Katrina, I toggled between CNN and the off button on the remote control. I could take only so much of the coverage but really had no desire to watch much of anything else. At one point I saw a man being interviewed on the front stoop of his home in New Orleans. He was one of the few who stayed and stayed and kept staying. His city had been ravaged, his home had been flooded, there was no drinking water, bodies were rotting in the streets, and these were his words as to why he wasn't willing to leave: "I can think of no better place they could take me than where I am right now."

I live for quotes like that. Especially ones this dense with spiritual irony: he couldn't say goodbye because he couldn't envision anything better. It's hard to get more myopic than that.

Leaving our false gods requires faith. We have to believe that where God wants to take us will be better than what we're clinging to, even if we can't imagine it. This man could only imagine what he had known, and even as it was crumbling around him he wanted the known over the unknown—even if the unknown was better.

Today we find the Israelites in a similar situation: They didn't want to leave the desert for the promised land.

> **Read Numbers 13:1-33.**
> **What did Moses want the 12 explorers to look for (vv. 17-20)?**
>
> **What did Moses ask them to do their best to bring back (v.20)?**
> ❏ the king captured alive   ❏ one of their idols
> ❏ dirt from the soil   ☒ fruit

I love this. Fruit from the land. This jumped out at me as a significant principle because fruit is used metaphorically all through Scripture. Jesus tells us in the New Testament that we can judge certain things by the fruit it yields—good or bad. Our lives are to bear fruit. God blesses us with spiritual fruit. Righteousness yields fruit.

> **Numbers 13:30, KJV**
> Caleb stilled the people before Moses, and said, Let us go up at once, and possess it; for we are well able to overcome it.

PERSONAL REFLECTION: Have you ever tasted or brought back fruit from a future promise that had not been fully realized? In other words, have you ever experienced a glimpse of what God promised you would eventually have in full? If so, describe your experience and whether or not it gave you the faith to keep pressing on.

Fill in the blank. Numbers 13:2 (NIV) says, "Send some men to explore the land of Canaan, which I am _giving_ to the Israelites."

Your Take: Is it perplexing to you that the Lord told Moses He was going to give the Israelites the land, but He wanted them to explore it first? At first glance, it seems to me that if He was going to give it to them, it would have been better for them to just go in there and take it. But the Lord wanted them to explore it first. Why do you think He wanted them to do this?

I'm sure there's an emphatic answer to this question, but I'm not sure I know it. It's possible that because God knows our strong ties to the familiar—even if it is a desert or a flooded house—He wanted them to see glimpses of the land so they would be more apt to go. Again, I'm not sure. I'd be interested to hear your opinions.

Looking only at verse 27, what report did the people come back with?
The land flowed with milk & honey

What's the first small but powerful word of verse 28?
The people are strong, the cities are fortified & large

The people were honest in their report of the land that flowed with milk, honey, and fruit, yet it was followed by the infamous word *but.* "But the people who live there are powerful, and the cities are fortified and very large." One thing I'm noticing here is that God's promises aren't necessarily realized without struggle.

I don't have this happen every day, but occasionally the Lord will give me a personal promise of which I'm absolutely convinced. I hesitate to even describe these experiences because I think specific words from God happen differently for different people. But the one thing I can definitely attest to is that often the ensuing events either seem contradictory to the promise or at least prove resistant. I might see the potential fruit, perhaps even taste it like the leaders of Israel, but I also come into contact with the proverbial giants and brick walls.

What obstacles are you currently experiencing in your pursuit of a promise God has given you? (It doesn't have to be a specific, personal promise—it can be a general one in Scripture you have struggled to grasp.) Write about it in the margin.

Continue reading Numbers 14:1-9. Do you think Joshua and Caleb saw the same physical characteristics of the land as the other 10 explorers? ☐ yes ☑ no

After seeing the land, what did Caleb and Joshua want to do, and what did the rest of the Israelites want to do?
Caleb & Joshua wanted to go in & take the land. The people wanted to go back to Egypt & was afraid.

From what I can tell, Joshua and Caleb saw all the same things. At no point did they contend with the others over the size of the people or the strength of their cities. What was remarkably different was their faith. Though they saw the strong people and the high walls, they believed the promise God had given them—that He would give them the land. They had faith that God would fulfill His promise despite the obstacles. This is just a question for you to ponder: Are the giants in your life causing you to disbelieve God and run to idols? Or are you holding to the promise He has given you, having faith that He can deal with your strongest opposition? If you're anything like me, it might be a little of both.

Draw a line between promises and fruit, and giants and walls. In the respective columns list the fruit and promises you are seeking to obtain opposite the connected giants and walls that have gotten in your way. After you've written, pray as you feel led. (One option is to pray for the faith to take hold of what God promises to give you, along with the faith that He will overcome what stands in your way.)

promises and fruit   **giants and walls**

Are the giants in your life causing you to disbelieve God and run to idols?

DAY 04 GOOD GOODBYES
THE RICH YOUNG RULER

**Mark 10:21
Jesus looked at him
and loved him.**

Today we near the end of the week with a passage from the New Testament. To get our minds rolling in the right direction, I've included a journal entry that Alli recently shared with me through e-mail. You're going to love it. It's so … Alli.

I have a hard time with change. I moved here five years ago from a medium-sized town in Iowa, and have just in the last year been able to use the words I love *in the same sentence as* Nashville. *It wasn't that I didn't like the city or enjoy the four years prior to this last one, but it was that I was here in body, and in Iowa in spirit.*

My husband and I are moving to a new house soon and have been purging our closets and cupboards of things we don't need or want. I was standing on the kitchen counter the other day digging through the top shelf of glasses and mugs, when I looked down at the pile of giveaways at my feet and saw two plastic juice glasses from my grandmother and a faded plastic Northern Iowa mug. I've tried to give these things away before but couldn't bring myself to do it because it felt like I was giving up a part of my Iowa past, a part of me.

All of the little physical things I was holding on to, like the glasses, were little metaphors of the way my heart was grabbing anything that represented home for me. Not that there's anything wrong with holding onto memorabilia, heirlooms, or things from my past. It's just that all the while I was praying that God would give me deep relationships here—would give me a home here—I felt like He was ignoring that prayer. I realize now that He was just waiting for me to make room in my heart for exactly that. I'm finding that when I dwell on a memory or a tradition in an unhealthy dose, it occupies every part of my brain that could otherwise be taking in my surroundings and what God may be trying to reveal to me. There is a place for sentimentality, but I've been a junkie, and living in the moment is a much fuller way to live.

I've been a junkie too, Alli. And on much deeper levels. Embracing the new and parting with things of the past have been impossible for me to do all by myself, which is why I love one of the verses we're looking at today: "With man this is impossible, but not with God; all things are possible with God" (Mark 10:27).

Read Mark 10:17-31. (If you're feeling industrious and can make extra time, read the other two passages of this same account in Mathew 19:16-30 and Luke 18:18-30. The way one personality sees things over another can touch us uniquely.)

There's a lot wrapped up in this story. I'll be candid with you: some of it I can explain and some of it is well beyond my biblical expertise. One thing I will note is that Jesus is not teaching that keeping the Ten Commandments and giving all you have to the poor will get you into heaven. He is not teaching that we gain our salvation by doing good works. In fact, He says the opposite. He made the case that no matter how good or perfect we think we are, we can never be good enough. No one is good enough to enter heaven, which is why Christ died on the cross to inherit our sin and penalty. It is also why He clearly stated that these things are impossible with men but possible with God.

Looking at verse 17, why did the rich young ruler approach Christ?

He wanted to how he could receive eternal life

Why do you think he walked away sad (v. 22)?

He did not want to give all his riches away.

Do you think he was sincere in his quest for eternal life?

❏ yes ☑ no

I think we can be sincere in our desire for the things of the Lord and still desire other things more. In this case, my own opinion is that the young ruler wanted eternal life with Christ, but he wanted his wealth more.

Look at verse 21 (NIV). Fill in the blank: "Jesus looked at him and __loved__ him."

Right after Jesus looked at the man with love, what did He say to him?

When it says that Jesus looked at him and loved him, I was almost expecting the next verse to say something like, so why don't you come to my house for a party, or let's go fishing on my new boat, or maybe we can play golf together on Saturday. Is anyone else surprised by His ensuing words?—You lack something; you need to sell all you have and give to the poor; then come follow me.

I'm not married, so I can only give examples with friends, but it has been my experience that when I tell someone I love them, it is usually best not to follow up with, "And by the way, let's talk about what is glaringly lacking in your life, and then perhaps we can spend a little time on how materialistic you are and how little you give to others." I realize that I'm over-emphasizing this here, but only to drive a point: God's love is so rich and refreshingly different than our often-limited views of love.

God's love is so rich and refreshingly different than our often-limited views of love.

Jesus looked at the young man with love, and His love drove Him to say in effect, "There's something you lack. You are missing treasure in heaven and you are unable to follow Me because something has a hold on you that is more important to you than Me. In your case, it is your wealth—it has to go."

This is love at its finest. What an encouraging picture! I believe many of us imagine God is looking down on us with an iron fist, telling us over and over where we need to improve so we can measure up. This account is strikingly different than that. It is the expressive eyes of Jesus looking at us and loving us enough to tell us what we lack. I find it interesting that Jesus told the young man that he was lacking something, and to remedy that lack he had to give something up—in essence, he had to lack more.

The Lord asks us to lose our life so we can find it. God offered great reward to the rich young ruler if he was willing to part with his idol of riches and follow Christ. Look at verses 29-30. What were those rewards?

Eternal life

Besides eternal life, when were all those rewards to be given?

When we get to heaven

Regardless of the deeper theological meanings of this text, I think it is safe to say that the rich young ruler not only would have received eternal life but also would have gained one hundred fold in his life on earth. I will tell you that I was especially moved by this verse: "Jesus looked at him and loved him" (v. 21). When the Lord tells us to part with our idols—or offer them up to Him—He is looking at us and loving us. He sees that our idols are in the way. He also knows that He has the power to turn whatever we parted with into a hundred fold in *this lifetime*, while also granting us eternal life. He can do this not because we make it possible, but because all things are possible with Him.

When the Lord tells us to part with our idols, He is looking at us and loving us.

Anadara recently discovered this in the midst of her move (all the nogs seem to be moving right now). She journaled the entry below. I thought her words might be a particularly good catalyst to some journaling for the rest of us.

I'm moving. This means I've also been cleaning out my house and finding pockets where I've been hiding things—come on, most of us know the ceremony of shoving things into closets when people come over. This is one way to clean. It would take too long to actually put things away and/or decide what to throw away, so we shove and close doors off to our company. I am guilty of doing this to Jesus. He showed me this as I was cleaning one day, but He did it in a loving way. It was not shameful. He gently pointed to corners of my closets and underneath my bed. He said, "I see this, and you know it's there too … though I think you've almost forgotten about it by now, it is still collecting major dust and is totally useless. It's taking up space. You have the illusion that it is still offering you something, or you have the hope that one day it will be of use to you. Come on, let's go clean it up."

Sometimes when I'm cleaning one thing I start to notice how dirty something else is … anyone relate? I get on cleaning sprees. The Lord has been doing this all over my life these last few years, and this study has been the kick-start to the making room. It has not happened overnight, but little by little I have begun to see change. I don't have to close off doors to the people in my life anymore. I can invite them in. Most important, I have invited Jesus into every room. Surprisingly, He's been helping me clean. I always imagined Him coming in and saying with an authoritative voice, "There's no room for Me here! When I come back this better be clean." (Hello moms everywhere.) Well, like a typical kid, with that kind of relationship with God, I just lived my life hiding the things I was supposed to get rid of and created the illusion that I had cleaned up.

I have come to find out, beautifully, that this is not how Jesus works. Jesus gets his hands dirty. He comes in and helps us clean. He hands us the things we need to get rid of. And He doesn't make a face. He doesn't complain. He is doing what He came to do. He is in His element. It is a gift to allow Him into the mess. It doesn't faze Him. He already knows it's there. But He wants us to clean with Him. We have to take part in it to understand the weight of what we have to clean out—and what we ultimately can't do by ourselves. Then we can truly appreciate it when He all of a sudden has room to sit down and start ministering to our hearts, truly providing for us the things we were ashamed of desiring—so we hid. All the things we were afraid we would lose. But we find out, when we lose our life we find it. Oh, the mystery.

I actually just finished moving. Thank goodness the nogs came to help pack my kitchen. Who knew we had been collecting so much stuff? I found myself saying, "Whose stuff is this unawares?" Seriously, the Lord has used this move to show me so much, so it's totally apropos that I'm sitting here in my new bedroom with my laptop and boxes all around, reading about "moving on and making room." This house was so roomy before we came in here with all our stuff. I almost told the movers to drive off when the truck was still half full. Goodness, we already had enough stuff in the house that I couldn't fathom what else was in that truck. I am thankful for all of our clothes, food, books, etc., but I am finally at a place where I understand the beauty of getting rid of the things that simply take up space. That's what our lesser gods do. They offer a false sense of security and hope. They really aren't doing anything. We are deceived.

The Lord comes in and makes the room in the house beautiful. Yes, it takes time to clean house, but don't think for a minute Jesus doesn't get His hands dirty with us. That's what He came and died for, to give us the freedom to say goodbye to the old and embrace the new. Jesus is passionate about invading every part of our hearts. He's not a taskmaster. He wants us to make room so He can come sit with us and minister to our hearts and be involved in every part of our life. As my view of God has been healed, I have had a much easier time inviting Him in to help me do housecleaning.

Like Anadara, the rich young ruler discovered he couldn't possibly part with all of his stuff on his own. But he didn't have to walk away sorrowful. That's where he had it wrong. He missed the life-saving fact that the One who asks us to clean house is the One who empowers us to do it. Perhaps that's why Luke 18:27 follows such an account: "The things which are impossible with men are possible with God" (KJV).

If today's study encouraged you to lay down something you are holding on to, write a prayer in the margin that includes the plea for God to do the impossible.

DAY 05 GOOD GOODBYES
ABRAHAM

I'm sitting on my couch this afternoon—which has turned into my desk—with my Bible and computer. I have such a hard time working in conventional settings with upright chairs and tables. It's so hard to take intermittent naps that way.

I've been mulling over principles we've mined from the Israelites and have decided I'm ready for some examples that are a bit more positive. Don't get me wrong; this past week we've seen some dear discoveries of God's loving character and graciousness to us. It's just that some of them have come from watching people who were doing it all wrong. Today we'll look at Abraham, who at least in this situation did it right.

Just to change things up a bit, let's start off today's reading with prayer. Take as much time as you need to be still before God. Reflect whatever is on your heart.

A.W. Tozer's *The Pursuit of God* is one of my all-time favorite books, and it contains a chapter entitled "The Blessedness of Possessing Nothing" that has to be one of my all-time favorite chapters in any book. Below is an excerpt from the chapter as it relates to Abraham and Isaac.

> Abraham was old when Isaac was born, old enough to have been his grandfather, and the child became at once the delight and idol of his heart. From the moment he first stooped to take the tiny form awkwardly in his arms, he was an eager love slave of his son. God went out of His way to comment on the strength of this affection. And it is not hard to understand. The baby represented everything sacred to his father's heart: the promises of God, the covenants, the hopes of the years and the long messianic dream. As he watched him grow from babyhood to young manhood, the heart of the old man was knit closer and closer with the life of his son, till at last the relationship bordered upon the perilous. It was then that God stepped in to save both father and son from the consequences of an uncleansed love.[1]

Genesis 22:12
Now I know that you fear God, because you have not withheld from me your son, your only son.

If you're familiar with the story of Abraham and Isaac, did you ever consider Isaac as an "idol" of Abraham's as Tozer refers to him? ☐ yes ☒ no

Read Genesis 22:1-18. If you're familiar with Scripture, it will be tempting to race through this account. But, as always, read thoughtfully, asking God to reveal Himself to you.

How did the angel know Abraham feared God (v. 12)?
Abraham was ready to slay Isaac.

Why did the angel say He would bless Abraham (vv. 16-17)?
Because Abraham had not withheld his son.

The last two questions have virtually the same answer: Abraham did not withhold his only son from the Lord. The word *withheld* jumped out at me during my reading of this passage. Consider it: the whole ordeal, the planning of the sacrifice, the three-day journey, the wood and fire, the fear and confusion Isaac must have experienced, the unspeakable grief and wonder Abraham must have gone through, and the angel appearing from heaven … all of it boiled down to this one word: *withheld*. In this case, he did *not* withhold his precious treasure from the Lord.

Part of what makes this whole study of "no other gods" so precious to me is its deeply-personal subject matter. I remember reading about Abraham and Isaac a few years ago while going through my own journey of having to lay certain things down. Huge things. Things I honestly didn't know if I could live without. The scary thing is that God asked me to lay them down before I knew whether or not I could live without them. Some of them He graciously gave back; others He did not. But in both cases, it was all for my good and His glory.

One thing that has greatly helped me through the "laying down" process is understanding the difference between letting something go and making it an offering. Abraham was laying Isaac down as an offering to the Lord. It wasn't something he threw on the altar and wiped his hands of, skipping down the mountain alone after he was done. The entire ordeal was an offering. I don't think we can miss this.

Just the other day I came home off a lonely week of travel. It was one of those times when I pretty much had to go straight to a Bible study I was teaching while my friends got together to eat dinner and watch Monday night football. I love football, I love my friends, and as you know by now, I'm crazy for food. But by the time I was done teaching my study, the party was over and I found myself alone yet again. Knowing that this is where God has me in my life, I lay on my bed and poured out my heart to the Lord. As I rehearsed my loneliness, I made it an offering to Him. I didn't deny my loneliness. I didn't just let it go. I offered it. It was something of a gift, knowing that I was putting the dearest parts of myself on an altar whose fragrance would reach the Lord Himself.

Consider another great quote from Tozer: "We are often hindered from giving up our treasures to the Lord out of fear for their safety ... But we need have no such fears. Our Lord came not to destroy but to save. Everything is safe which we commit to Him, and nothing is really safe which is not so committed."[2]

Is there something the Lord is asking you to no longer withhold from Him? ❑ yes ❑ no

If your answer is yes, list in the margin the reasons you are afraid to give it over to Him.

Wrapping up, reread verses 13-18. If you're afraid to relinquish control of certain things to the Lord I hope the fact that God is referred to here as Jehovah-Jireh—"the Lord Will Provide"— brings you a certain amount of relief. Provision is part of His nature. Also, I hope you noted the fact that God brought huge blessings on Abraham as a result of his obedience.

I firmly believe that Satan, certain strands of our culture, and our own fears keep us from offering our dearest treasures to the Lord. If you're like me, you're certain that the minute you pray that prayer you'll be sent to Africa to live in a hut as a missionary; God will make you fall in love with your weirdest, most unattractive, single neighbor; or you'll have to sell all you have and live on ramen noodles for the rest of your life. I'm here to hold up verses 13-18 as a much more reliable standard as to what can happen when we give our all to the Lord.

I've looped the following song by Anadara about a thousand times over the past few months. If you're at a place of surrender, this song is the perfect backdrop. You can grab it off the Web site if you want, or just prayerfully read the words here.

"Everything is safe which we commit to Him, and nothing is really safe which is not so committed."
—A.W. Tozer

Heard a song that spoke to you during your study this week? Share it on the discussion boards at: http//www.lifeway.com/livingroomseries

SONG OF MY SURRENDER [3]
FATHER, RICH IN MERCY
RADIANT WITH GLORY
I SUBMIT MY WILL TO ALL YOUR WAYS
THERE'S NO DARKNESS AROUND YOU
I AM LOST WITHOUT YOU
LEAD AND LIGHT MY PATH ALL OF MY DAYS

CHORUS:
LET THE NIGHT BOW TO THE SUN
LET THE DAY LIKE FREEDOM COME
LORD YOU ARE THE LIGHT OF ALL THE WORLD
CAN THE CLAY RISE UP AND STAND
WITHOUT THE POTTER'S GUIDING HAND?
THIS IS THE SONG OF MY SURRENDER
THIS IS THE SONG OF MY SURRENDER

MIGHTY KING AND SAVIOR
FROM THIS MOMENT I'M YOURS
WRITE YOUR NAME ON EVERY PART OF ME
FERVENTLY I WILL SEEK YOU
DESPERATELY I NEED YOU
MOLD ME INTO WHO I'M MEANT TO BE

CHORUS

If you're ready to lay one thing or a few things down, I will leave you with the very prayer I've prayed a few monumental times in my life. Again, A.W. Tozer wrote it. I just haven't found anyone who says it more precisely or more eloquently: "Father, I want to know Thee, but my cowardly heart fears to give up its toys. I cannot part with them without inward bleeding, and I do not try to hide from Thee the terror of the parting. I come trembling, but I do come. Please root from my heart all those things which I have cherished so long and which have become a very part of my living self, so that Thou mayest enter and dwell there without a rival. Then shalt Thou make the place of Thy feet glorious. Then shall my heart have no need of the sun to shine in it, for Thyself wilt be the light of it, and there shall be no night there. In Jesus' name. Amen."[4]

1. A. W. Tozer, *The Pursuit of God* (Camp Hill, PA: Christian Publications, 1993), 24.
2. Ibid., 28
3. Written by Anadara Arnold, Joe Beck, Billy Sprague. Copyright 2005 All For The King Music/Postage Stamp Publishing (admin. By The Loving Company)/ Hallal Music/Skin Horse, Inc. (ASCAP)/Willow branch Music (admin. By Gaither Copyright Mgmt.)/Yada, Yada, Yada Music (BMI).
4. Tozer, 30.

SICILIAN PIZZA CRUST
PREHEAT OVEN TO 400°–425° SERVES 6

Perhaps it's been a rough week for you. May I suggest the ultimate comfort food? Nothing like a little pizza to help ease the sting.

1½ c. warm water (see note)
1 pkg. dry yeast
3 T. olive oil
1½ tsp. salt
1 tsp. sugar
4 c. white flour
¼ c. olive oil

Dissolve yeast in warm water. Add next three ingredients (through sugar). Stir. Then add 2 of the cups of flour. (I beat it with my mixer, but you don't have to. You can mix with a wooden spoon.) Then add the other 2 cups, one at a time, mixing in. Knead it until it is smooth, about 5 minutes. Place in an olive oil greased bowl, brush top with olive oil, and cover with a damp cloth. Place in a warm place for about an hour. (I heat the oven just a little, then turn it off, and put it in there. Just be careful it's not too hot so the dough doesn't start cooking.) After it is risen, punch it down and lightly roll it onto the pizza pan. Brush with the remaining olive oil if desired. Let rise again an hour. (You can omit this step if you wish.)

Once dough has risen to your satisfaction, cover with your favorite pizza toppings. (I especially like tomato sauce, roma tomatos, basil, and mozzarella.) Then place in 400-425 degree preheated oven and cook for approximately 10 minutes. This time varies considerably depending on the oven. Look for melted cheese and a golden brown crust.

Note: The water that is added to the yeast should be quite warm, almost hot, but not so hot that it burns you. If it's not hot enough, the dough won't rise. If it is too hot, then it kills the yeast!

SESSION 06
GOD OF GODS
THE SOUTH AND THE SPHINX

I AM RIDICULOUSLY HAPPY IN NASHVILLE. AT LEAST TODAY.

RIGHT NOW IT'S NOVEMBER, IT'S A STUNNING 70 DEGREES, THE BRILLIANTLY-COLORED LEAVES ARE STILL GRASPING THEIR BRANCHES, AND THE SKY IS A STRIKING BLUE. IN FACT, I WISH I HAD A T-SHIRT IN THIS PARTICULAR SHADE OF SKY. I'VE MADE SOME PRETTY AMAZING FRIENDSHIPS HERE—THE KIND OF FRIENDSHIPS YOUR HEART ALWAYS HOLDS OUT HOPE FOR, BUT THAT YOU'RE NOT SURE YOU'LL EVER FIND. THEY AREN'T PERFECT FRIENDSHIPS, BUT THEY ARE LIFELONG, DEEP, AND FULL OF WHATEVER SAYS "HOME."

I've also inherited a couple of my friend's golden retrievers in the process, Max and Chloe. I don't have to raise them; I just get to be the fun aunt who has treats in her cupboard and happens to live near a park where they can frolic on an occasional morning. Right now, Max is contentedly sitting beside me while rays of sunshine cast themselves across his red coat. It's the little things. I'm having a great day here. And given my melancholy nature, I have to highlight these days when they come.

Yesterday was a great day too, for reasons that may be specific only to me, but I'll share them anyway. After moving from jam-packed—albeit amazing—Washington D.C., where every restaurant has a minimum wait of two hours, where you can't leave your house between five and nine in the morning or three and eight in the evening (unless you enjoy serpentine lines of traffic), and where the malls are teeming with so many people you have to walk sideways, I have come to emphatically appreciate the smaller city of Nashville. It's a place where people say "hi" and it doesn't take 45 minutes to get across the street. For the most part, customer service is decent and if you go to a restaurant for dinner you can usually be seated that same night.

All these things said, though, I'm not sure anything has topped the experience I had here yesterday while getting my car inspected and buying a new battery. You first need to know that I absolutely hate lines. I know no one likes them, but I almost have nervous breakdowns in them. I would rather have my teeth drilled than stand in a line. I strategize

myself out of lines. I plan my life around avoiding them. That is precisely why I have always dreaded getting my car inspected, because where I grew up in Virginia it felt like an all-day ordeal. How many times I pulled up to the emissions station and had to make that awful choice of which line to get in.

I don't know why I labored over the decision so hard, because it was a proven fact that whichever line I chose would be the slowest. Even if I chose the line I wasn't going to choose in hopes of tricking the system, it was still the slowest. So imagine my surprise when yesterday I pulled up to the station here in Nashville and there were no cars in front of me! Within mere moments my car had gone through the test—failing, but that was no matter. The pure, unadulterated joy of not having to wait made up for such superfluous details. I rejoiced in my city as I drove away.

Next stop, getting my battery changed. If there's something I loathe just slightly less than lines, it's dealing with car issues. It seems no matter how new your car is, there's always some part that's "just about to go." But, alas, I've found a functioning battery is not optional, so I pulled up to the nearest service station and met an elderly mechanic named Jackie.

I told him I needed a battery switched out, to which he pleasantly replied, "Pop the hood, ma'am." I reached for the lever only to find that the hood wouldn't disengage. This escalated into a far bigger problem than the battery. Apparently there was some rust on the latches, which I think means more lines in my future. Twenty-five minutes later, Jackie had the hood open, and another twenty after that, he had my battery in. All in all, I suppose I was there a little under an hour.

By Northern Virginia standards, I was expecting to swipe my card for a hefty sum—especially after the hood incident. I couldn't have been more perplexed when the woman at the counter charged me five dollars and seventy-five cents. I think I wept on the gas station counter. Two minutes in the inspection line and five dollars for an installed battery! I will never leave this town! I found Jackie in the back of the garage and handed him some extra cash, thanking him profusely. I jumped in my emissions-failed Jeep and drove off with a warm heart, basking in the kindness and affordability of the South.

This is all coming from the same girl who swore she would never leave Northern Virginia. I thrived in the fast-paced environment and enjoyed the politics and cosmopolitan flair. I took for granted the ability to pop into the city for the day and sit in the Air and Space Museum with 3D glasses on in front of a towering screen that took you to the moon and back in 30 minutes. Since moving to Nashville I have occasionally missed those things, along with authentic Thai restaurants, a myriad of foreign accents, and IKEA.

All this is probably why I recently felt an especially strong tug to check out the Egyptian exhibit at Nashville's Frist Museum. I saw it as a chance to embrace a little of what I missed about D.C.

I talked Alli into going with me, which wasn't too hard since she's far more hip than I am and has a season pass. We had quite a time following one another around with headsets and MP3 players that gave us the history of each piece. I can't remember what was our favorite, though I do recall us tarrying over a mummified cat that looked strangely like a hotdog. The things they hung onto.

Though the cat was up there, I did have a monumental experience that I doubt I'll ever forget. It was one of the first things Alli and I saw when entering the room. In front of us stood a towering statue in the form of a sphinx holding out the symbol of life. The British voice in my headset said that the Egyptians would bow down before this exact statue, hoping that life would be extended to them.

As I took notice of every detail, I remember thinking how I couldn't imagine anyone would ever believe that this lifeless form of rock could do anything, much less give life. I remember thinking how strange it hit me, and how I could never see myself doing that. The next words I heard cross through my head were, *You do it all the time.* I knew they were Holy Spirit words the moment I heard them. They weren't audible, but they were definitive. If you can hear a silent voice, I heard this one. *Lord, I would never look for life from something like this,* I silently answered.

But you look for life from lesser things than Me all the time, every day.

I was struck. Frozen, I stood before this idol, suddenly aware of the fact that all the things I had placed my full hope in were not a hair more able. Suddenly I realized that I had been looking to weak things, even good things, for life, which Christ alone can give. It was a freeing moment.

I love when the Holy Spirit speaks to me like this. It wasn't condemning; it was simply enlightening. It was convicting—the freeing kind I wrote about earlier in our study. This conviction demanded my repentance while extending the truth that God wanted me to trust Him for far more. I talked Alli's ear off about it on the way home. I am so happy to always remember that day with her as part of it.

I love when God speaks to me in these ways. It reminds me of how deeply He is engaged in my life and how He desires for me to find my life in Him, not in people, dreams, agendas, drinking, career paths, food, sex, or a litany of other things that we substitute for Him. Though we have all looked to the lesser, this week our focus is on the God of gods. He is the only reason behind this journey. So … lay your sphinx aside and make room.

DAY 01 GOD OF GODS
ULTIMATE SATISFACTION

If I could change anything about the way I experienced Christianity as a kid, I would probably reverse something. I would switch the percentage of time (I'm guessing about 90%) spent focusing on all the "bad" things in my life that weren't supposed to be there with the 10% spent focusing on Christ. I fear we have this terribly backward. We spend too much time trying to rid ourselves of rebellion, lust, jealousy, materialism, drug addictions, and whatever other idols rule our lives, while spending this miniscule amount of time on knowing the One True God.

In light of this, I am looking forward to turning our attentions away—for a bit—from the gods that rule us to the only God who has given His Son so that we might be in relationship with Him.

The great English preacher Spurgeon put it this way:

> If thou hast anything that perplexes thee, the simplest plan for thee will be, not to try to solve the difficulty, but to seek direction from heaven concerning it. If thou hast, at this moment, some doubt that is troubling thee, thy wisest plan will be, not to combat the doubt, but to come to Christ just as thou art, and to refer the doubt to him. Remember how men act when they are concerned in a lawsuit; if they are wise, they do not undertake the case themselves. They know our familiar proverb, "He who is his own lawyer has a fool for his client"; so they take their case to someone who is able to deal with it, and leave it with him.[1]

Before going any further, present yourself to God, leaving all your struggles, issues, and doubts with Him. He is able.

One of my friends owns a guitar shop. She recently asked me if I'd take an 11-hour road trip with her to pick up 28 high-end guitars from a private collector and player who was liquidating his stash. Because I'm a sucker for expensive guitars, I obliged, jumped in a cargo van, and took off. We arrived at the man's house yesterday morning and

Isaiah 55:1
Come, all you who are thirsty, come to the waters; and you who have no money, come, buy and eat! Come, buy wine and milk without money and without cost.

anxiously began flipping latches to see what each guitar case held. The owner (who was a bit odd—I just need to get this out there) would point to a case and say, "I paid over $6,000 for this one, but I've never seen it." Thinking I misunderstood him, I replied, "You mean you've never played it?"

"No, I've never seen it. I've had it two years and I've never even opened the case," he said. On the outside I was smiling, but on the inside the phrase *this guy's weird* kept running through my head. This was pretty much the situation for about half the guitars he owned.

This kind of stuff really intrigues me: to have over $100,000 worth of guitar inventory that you've never even seen, forget about played. Because this is how I always think, I couldn't help but mull over the obvious metaphor: how many spiritual guitar cases do I have that I've never even opened, much less played?

Forgive me if this is cheesy, but sometimes I can't avoid analogies like these. But you know what I'm saying? We have all these treasures in the Lord. We have all these promises. Right at our fingertips we have the God who knows every falling star and stirs up every wave and mends broken hearts. We have His written Word that sits buried under *Cosmopolitan*. Many who consider themselves Christians barely open the Word, and I would contend even more open it but never play. I'm hoping over the next few weeks we can discover what we've always owned—all God has to offer. And most important, I hope we play.

> **Read Isaiah 55:1-9. It's about that time for me to be annoying and remind you to read slowly and thoughtfully.**
>
> **What kind of people is the Lord calling to come to Him?**
>
> *Thirsty people, hungry people, no money.*

Let your answer sink in: those who are thirsty; those who have no money (or, I believe it's safe to say, those who are poor in any way—be it relationally poor, financially poor, physically poor, and so forth).

> **How much do the wine and milk of the Lord cost?**
>
> *Nothing.*

> Right at our fingertips we have the God who knows every falling star and stirs up every wave and mends broken hearts.

According to the end of verse 2 (NIV), how do we know God is not necessarily talking about physical bread, wine, and milk?

Soul

"And your soul will delight in the richest of fare." God is talking about soul food here. He is saying that our souls don't need to starve anymore. And isn't starvation one of the main reasons propelling us to false gods? We yearn for attention but don't get it the way we want, so we soothe our ache by losing ourselves in television. We get angry, so we turn to the god of alcohol and drown our sorrows. We long for intimacy, so we satiate our desire with pornography. We are lonely, so we overeat to fill the void. We feel worthless, so we put in 90-hour workweeks to make us feel valuable. The list is endless, and yet none of it satiates.

PERSONAL REFLECTION: Write below any way your soul is hungry and thirsty. Be specific. For me, I'll tell you that recently my soul has been afraid. I have needed the food of peace. I've written more specifically in my journal. Your turn …

What does God ask in the beginning of Isaiah 55:2?

Why do you spend money on things that do not satisfy?

Ughhhhhhhhhh. (That is the typed version of me groaning right now.) How much time and energy I have spent over the years trying to grasp what does not ultimately satisfy. I have spun so many wheels, maneuvered, balanced on a wire, tried to keep plates spinning, spent my resources … all for what I thought would satisfy but didn't. God's question makes me groan because just the fact that He has to ask a question like this seems so ridiculous, and yet it is perfectly apt.

It's interesting that God says, "Why do you spend money on what is NOT bread?" I think this is a clear reference to false gods. The Lord is inferring that what they thought they were buying was bread, but really it was not. Obviously we wouldn't run after false gods if we didn't think on some level they would deliver. We want bread, so we go after what we think is bread. But how often it proves to be a counterfeit. How often we end up laboring for something that didn't deliver what we thought, because it wasn't what we thought.

PERSONAL REFLECTION: Answer God's question you wrote on the last page.

My prayer for you and my prayer for me is that we wouldn't be like the guitar collector (not just because he was weird)—totally unaware of what he had. We have the God of the universe who is calling the hungry, calling the thirsty, calling those in need to come and delight in the richest of fare. Do you believe it? Do you believe God when He says He can satisfy you? Take just a moment to ponder how strong your belief is in God's offer.

> **Hold your thought and read Romans 9:30-32. The Israelites didn't obtain righteousness because they lacked …**
> ☒ **faith**　❏ **good works**　❏ **sacrifices**　❏ **holiness**

> **Keeping in mind where your own level of faith is, read Hebrews 12:2.**　*Jesus is where my faith is.*

Jesus Christ is the author and finisher of our faith.

Jesus Christ is the author and finisher of our faith. So if we are lacking faith in His ability to delight our soul with the richest of fare, I propose that all we need to do is ask. Many people in the New Testament asked God to increase their faith or help their unbelief. Hebrews 11:6 says that without faith it is impossible to please God. God would not ask something of us that He wouldn't equip us to accomplish.

> **Finish by writing a prayer about experiencing God's deep satisfaction. I am doing the same, because the Lord currently has me in a situation I don't understand and have no idea how to change or resolve. I want to please Him with a faith that believes He will satisfy my soul, though the places that once brought satisfaction are dried up for the moment. Perhaps that is the point … that I would come to Him who satisfies … freely.**

128

DAY 02 GOD OF GODS
AN INVITATION

I really don't like to do things twice. Just last week I went through the hassle of taking everything out of my room and painting the walls what I thought was a deep brown with a hint of red. After all, that's what the handy two-by-two-inch color card suggested. Turns out it was more of a deep red with a hint of brown.

By the way, who in the world thought those little squares up? Like you can tell anything about what a room with all its furniture and lighting and color themes is going to look like from a paper square. I think the whole thing is a marketing device. Every day there are thousands of us all over the world holding up little pallets on our walls going, *Now this is gonna look great.* Ten hours later we're back in line with another misleading square purchasing another color (root of bitterness, root of bitterness).

Needless to say, we don't always get what we think we're getting. What we've envisioned and what we actually come away with can be two totally different things—as evidenced by the four coats of paint on my bedroom wall. My friend Scott is convinced I've lost square footage.

The principle of the deceptive color card also holds true at the table of our idols. We come to them hoping they will provide us with what's on the paint square in our minds, but we rarely end up with what we expected—which is why I want us to revisit Isaiah 55:1-9.

Sometimes revisiting things that we think we've already mined to death can offer surprising nuggets we didn't see the first time. Don't rush through it because you read it yesterday. (I only say this because it's my own tendency.) Ask God to reveal new things to you: Scripture is dense enough, and He can do it.

> **Isaiah 55:9**
> As the heavens are higher than the earth, so are my ways higher than your ways and my thoughts than your thoughts.

> **Reread Isaiah 55:1-9. List below all the action words and phrases that God was asking of the Israelites. Repeat them if they are mentioned more than once. I'll start you off: come, come …**
>
> *buy, eat, come, buy, eat, listen, incline, come hear, seek, call, return,*

Our soul delights in God when we come, listen, turn from our idols, and call out to Him.

This was an enlightening exercise for me. To see words, some of them multiple times, such as come, hear, listen, call, turn, and seek helped me better understand how to satiate my soul with the richest of fare. Our soul does not delight in God over a Scripture-memory verse or church attendance or doing a Bible study alone. It delights in Him when we come, listen, turn from our idols, and call out to Him.

Simply put, this is relationship. Coming to Him, hearing from Him, putting other things aside that get in the way, and speaking back to Him—all of these make up the ingredients for intimacy with another, in this case with God.

I love Lauri. She goes a mile a minute and can articulate more words in twenty seconds than anyone I've ever heard. She would have been a good auctioneer, but we'll gladly take her as a make-up artist and actress. A few weeks ago she mentioned that it was hard for her to sit quietly before the Lord. She admitted to getting fidgety and said she starts thinking about ten other things. All of us around the dinner table were nodding like we know all too well. She's just someone who's not afraid to say it, which I appreciate.

For most of us—active or passive, driven or laid back, open or private—sitting quietly before the Lord (that would be the come part), listening to Him, and calling on Him do not come naturally. We have to work at it. But the more we do it, the more we find it not only satiating but absolutely essential.

I want to highlight verses 7-9 of our reading. Perhaps you've already been blessed by this passage. I love how God says He will have mercy on us and will freely pardon us when we return to Him. He follows this up by saying, "My thoughts are not your thoughts, and your ways are not My ways ... as heaven is higher than earth, so My ways are higher than your ways" (vv. 8-9, HCSB).

We're not used to being extended mercy and we're not used to being pardoned freely. But God's ways are beyond ours. This is how He operates when we turn from our sin and return to Him. If you have something that you know is obstructing your relationship with the Lord, take time to verbalize it to Him, turn from it, and thank Him that He pardons freely. I'm letting this truth bless me freshly today, for my heart has been very dark at times. I praise Him that His ways are not like mine. I praise Him that His pardons are free.

I thought we'd do things a bit differently today. Since we just spent time turning from anything we needed to put behind us, we're going to take a psalm and practice the other three parts of coming to Him, listening to Him, and calling on Him.

You'll have a choice of what psalm you want to meditate on based on where you are in your life right now. Here are the options—unless you have another psalm you really want to read.

If you're…

going through a difficult time, read Psalm 116.

going through a season of joy and thanksgiving, read Psalm 145.

needing confession and restoration, read Psalm 51.

struggling with identity and self-worth, read Psalm 139.

in a time of crisis, read Psalm 143.

needing wisdom and instruction (and have a bunch of time), read Psalm 119.

longing for intimacy with God, read Psalm 42.

wanting wisdom and encouragement, read Psalm 37.

wanting to be reminded of God's greatness and power, read Psalm 18.

Before you read your psalm, take a moment to sit quietly as a visible act of your coming to Him. As you begin reading, listen to what He is telling you through His written Word. Finally, call out to Him in whatever way you are wanting. Write below about what you heard and how you responded. I'm about to do the same. My prayer is that together we will delight in the richest of fare.

DAY 03 GOD OF GODS
PROVISION

Genesis 22:13
Abraham looked
up and there in a
thicket he saw a
ram caught by its
horns. He went over
and took the ram
and sacrificed it as
a burnt offering
instead of his son.

Today my hope is that we will find true relationship with the Lord and that His anointing will be on our pursuit of leaving behind functional gods while apprehending God Himself. I want revelation for us: those moments where we have no doubt that God is speaking—where suddenly a black and white text becomes a life-transforming revelation in our specific lives in our specific circumstances. I pray this happens as we look at a passage we looked at a few weeks ago—but this time from a different angle.

From the vantage point of laying our idols down, we read about Abraham offering up Isaac. The discussion hit a lot of chords in our group. As I was praying about today's study, the word *provision* ran across my mind. At least in my own life, one of the central things I am looking for from my functional gods is provision. This is often why they are so hard to let go of—after all, what, then, will provide for me in their place? Is God truly enough? Can His provision fill all the vacant spaces where my idols once lived? These are my questions … perhaps they are yours as well.

> **Look back at Genesis 22:1-19, keeping the concept of provision in mind. Write below the phrase that contains the first mention of the word *provide*. In that written phrase, circle what Abraham said God would provide.**

lamb

> **What does verse 13 say God provided?**
> ❑ a lamb   ❑ an ox   ☒ a ram   ❑ no sacrifice needed

I love that right in the midst of Abraham's agony of having to slay his most precious possession, he looked up and right before him was a ram caught by his horns in the thicket—provision was literally caught in front of him. As is already obvious to you, this is not exactly the way Abraham thought things were going to work out. He told Isaac that God would provide a lamb. But read Hebrews 11:17-19 and see how the window opens even wider into his limited foresight.

What do these verses say Abraham reasoned God would do?

God could raise Isaac from the dead.

Now go back to Genesis 22 and read verse 5. Abraham told his servants that he and the _son_ would go, worship, and come back to them.

With all of these pieces on the table, we get enough of a picture to see Abraham believed that somehow God was going to provide. God had already told him that his seed would come through Isaac, so though Abraham didn't understand how God could tell him that by following it up with a command to slay the very same son, he figured that God would provide and that He could raise the dead if He had to.

Isn't it interesting that Abraham was wrong about the process but right in concept? This is the kind of wrong that is perfectly OK to be. He was wrong about the details but right about the fact that God would provide. God honored his faith, never giving a thought to Abraham's superfluous errors of how it would happen.

I find it interesting that Abraham had to prepare for something that logically didn't make any sense to him. He had to gather the servants, cut the wood, load the donkey, find the place of sacrifice, and so forth. And yet none of it added up. The only thing he could half conclude was that God could raise the dead and that He would provide a lamb. Ultimately, Abraham believed God to be a God of provision.

> **PERSONAL REFLECTION:** Are you currently going through a time when you really have no idea how things are going to work out, but you are moving ahead in faith, believing that God will show Himself as the Lord who provides? Write your complexities out before the Lord. Pray for the faith of Abraham, who might have had the details wrong but had God as Jehovah-Jireh so perfectly right. (If you don't have anything like this going on, spend time thanking God for His many provisions.)

DAY 04 GOD OF GODS
CHOICE

Exodus 3:14
God said to Moses,
"I AM WHO I AM.
This is what you are
to say to the Israel-
ites: 'I AM has sent
me to you.'"

I think that we make God very small in our western Christian culture. I know I do, and I don't want to. I can't tell you how many times I've thought of Barry and all those guitar cases he had never opened, housing all those guitars he had never played. I guess there were too many other things going on in his life that stole his attention.

One obstacle he mentioned was that he was a perfectionist and basically didn't want to play if he couldn't be great. (If you've ever seen me playing guitar, you know this has never stopped me.) He was too afraid to pursue something he wasn't sure he would be successful at. So as a result, Brazilian Rosewood guitars with abalone inscriptions built by genius luthiers sat individually encased in his basement for years. Never seen, never touched, never played. But what are our excuses? Are we afraid to find out who God really is? Are we skeptical? Complacent? Is too much else competing for our time? Are we afraid God won't love us? Are we content with how things are and too afraid of what might happen if we play?

In our culture there are myriad lures competing for our time and attention. I was reminded of this while reading through James and thought it would be good to look at it more closely.

> Read James 4:1-10.
>
> Read Matthew 6:24.
>
> Compare James 4:4 with Matthew 6:24. List the similarities in concept below. (Don't feel like you have to totally understand the concepts of the verses to list their similarities.)

Desires of the heart - fights & wars
Friend of the world - enemy of God.

> Why are we not instructed to separate ourselves from people of the world (see 1 Cor. 5:9-10)?

So, they will not influence us to worldly things.

Paul clearly states that separating ourselves from people outside our faith would require we leave the world (some of them are hoping for this). Throughout Scripture we see Jesus, His disciples, and significant women mingling and loving people in "the world." So, clearly this is not the kind of friendship James is talking about.

> **Keeping this in mind, go back to James 4:4 and write what you think "friendship with the world" means.**
>
> *Friendship with the devil.*

> **Your Take: What do you think Jesus meant in Matthew 6:24 when He said we "cannot be slaves of God and of money"?**
>
> *What you love controls you.*

After further nosiness, I found out Barry was selling his guitar collection to make room for his vintage pipe collection. I saw this as a good move on his part since pipe cases take up a lot less room, a positive thing if you're not worried about cancer of the mouth. Guitar playing lost out to pipe smoking for Barry, and the guitars had to go. I'm thinking this is a little of what Jesus meant when He said we can't serve both God and money. And what James meant when he said we couldn't be friends with God and the world.

It's not that we can't have money (or fill-a-false-god-in-the-blank) or that we can't love things in the world. Scripture even says God has given us all things to enjoy. It's a lot more about which one is our master. In the NIV, Matthew 6:24 says we can't serve both God and money (both God and our idols). I think the same principle carries over into what James was saying about friendship—we can't have ultimate allegiance to both God and the world. Barry had only enough love and space for one pursuit. He couldn't service collecting both guitars and pipes. Just the same, we can't serve two masters. Any idol in our lives becomes our master.

> **Look back at James 4:5. What does it say that the Spirit within us does?**
>
> *Yearns jealously*

I kind of like this. It sort of fires me up that God's Spirit envies so intensely in us. He simply will not allow our allegiance to be elsewhere.

For starters, it shows us we're deeply cared for. I'm glad God is not passively sitting back in my heart thinking, *Oh, she's going for the*

> We can't have ultimate allegiance to both God and the world.

chocolate cake again, or the explicit movie, or to her boyfriend's for the night—too bad I can't compete with that.

Sometimes I wish I could get away with something. But He won't have it, because He's too great, too holy, too righteous, and has too much to offer to let us serve anything less than Him.

As I said earlier in the week, I want to focus on God's greatness. We can't expect to turn from our idols if we have nothing to turn to. We'll close today by looking at one of the first names God gave Himself in the Old Testament; it expresses this greatness.

Flip to Exodus 3:14. What is the name God gives Himself?

I Am

Commentator Matthew Henry describes the name I AM as follows:

> A name that denotes what he is in himself, I AM THAT I AM.
> This explains his name Jehovah, and signifies,
> 1. That he is self-existent: he has his being of himself.
> 2. That he is eternal and unchangeable, and always the
> same, yesterday, to-day, and for ever.
> 3. That he is incomprehensible; we cannot by searching find
> him out: this name checks all bold and curious inquiries
> concerning God.
> 4. That he is faithful and true to all his promises,
> unchangeable in his word as well as in his nature; let Israel
> know this, I AM hath sent me unto you. I am, and there is
> none else besides me. All else have their being from God,
> and are wholly dependent upon him. Also, here is a name
> that denotes what God is to his people.[2]

At the end of the day it's between I AM and everything else. Because we cannot serve both, I thought it would be telling to compare and contrast our prominent functional god versus THE GREAT I AM. My goal is that we'll walk away with greater allegiance to the latter. Write your comparisons below.

At the end of the day it's between I AM and everything else.

DAY 05 GOD OF GODS
BOWING DOWN

We just had dinner at Carrie's, whose place I love. She's one of those people who can take five bucks and create a room straight out of *Dwell* magazine. Her house imbues warmth and her cooking is just ridiculous. She's always making up recipes and forgetting to write them down for the rest of us mortals. (Lauri's the same way—I can't get a recipe out of her for anything.) For me, this kind of environment spawns thought, conversation, and creativity; we always have great discussions at Carrie's. Last week was no exception.

I threw out the question: "Have you ever had an experience with a physical idol, as spoken about more specifically in the Old Testament?" Carrie had traveled to India and therefore had several thoughts to share. What surprised me was what Alli had experienced in our own backyard. I asked her to write down what she shared that night:

When I first moved to Nashville, the restoration of a replica of the Parthenon was being completed. One of the main attractions inside the structure is a 41-foot 10-inch statue of the Greek goddess Athena. Now she is painted gold and green and all sorts of shiny colors, but the first time I visited she was still completely white. It was a weekday and there weren't many people there. (I'm telling you this to somehow justify my experience, because I don't want you to think I'm totally weird.)

When I walked into the enormous room housing Athena, I was very surprised at how I felt. I was immediately drawn to the beauty of the statue and think I might have even held my breath. Someone could have been yelling my name behind me and I wouldn't have noticed. What I felt was a moment of awe. It wasn't like seeing Niagara Falls or the Rocky Mountains because I've never felt compelled to bow down before nature.

In that moment I understood the desire to worship statues and felt this small urge to drop to my knees. She was so tangible and beautiful and made me feel small and less worthy. It was an odd feeling that scared me but also allowed me to understand some things more fully. I am not unlike the

Isaiah 46:4
I have made you and I will carry you; I will sustain you and I will rescue you.

wayward Israelites and have moments when I just want to worship something I can photograph. I also realized that if a statue built by humans can make me feel that way even for a second, I can't imagine what it will feel like to be in the full presence of the God who built creation.

I love Alli's honesty. I suppose that has been one of the more brilliant parts of our gatherings—the freedom to be authentic, to share with candor. I always walk away from our times together feeling a sense of normalcy. Not because I find Lauri, Anadara, Alli, or Carrie particularly normal, but actually because I find the same quirks and struggles in their lives as in my own. So it's ironically the lack of normalcy that makes me feel normal. Get it? My point is, I appreciated Alli opening up this way because it reminds me of the times I've been taken in by certain things, apart from God, that have elicited my plain and simple worship.

As we end our week I want to go out with the characteristics and nature of God strong in our hearts. When we see Him for who He is, the strength of our idols lose their pull.

> When we see God for who He is, the strength of our idols lose their pull.

Before reading the following passage, ask that God reveal something of Himself that you have yet to see.

Read Isaiah 44:6-8 and list all the ways God describes Himself.

This God's blessing on Israel and describes what God will do to Israel. First & last & no other Gods.

Read Isaiah 46:1-2. *Dead idols, have to carry*

PERSONAL REFLECTION: Verse 1 speaks of the idols as being burdensome for people who are already weary. It speaks of these idols as drawing people off into captivity. If you can identify, describe how your current (or previous) functional gods have been burdensome to you.

Now read Isaiah 46:3-5.

To remember what God has done is so important. Whether we've been Christ followers for most of our lives or just a few weeks, we each have our own story of how God has carried and sustained us.

Without going into lots of detail, simply jot down some bullet points of the ways God has sustained and blessed you over the years. You can go back as early as your birth.

I want to end today's study by doing something we haven't done before. I want us to physically bow down before the Lord with our Bibles and study spread out in front of us. I want us to worship God for the attributes we listed about Him from Isaiah 44:6-8. I want us to worship Him for the ways we recounted He has sustained, blessed, and rescued us. I want us to worship Him for being the God who saves, unlike our idols who only burden us.

I want us to worship Him for being the God who saves, unlike our idols who only burden us.

I just finished this act of worship. The reason I had my Bible in front of me was because I prayed back the different Scriptures that especially ministered to me. For instance, from Isaiah 46:4, I prayed back, "Lord, You have made me, You will carry me, You will sustain and rescue me."

End this week in prayer. End this week bowing down. End this week in worship of the God of gods.

---

1. C.H. Spurgeon, "Sweet Stimulants for the Fainting Soul," Bible Bulletin Board, http://www.biblebb.com/files/spurgeon/2798.htm (accessed April 23, 2007).
2. Matthew Henry, *Matthew Henry's Concise Commentary on the Whole Bible* (Nashville: Thomas Nelson, 1997), 78-79.

GRANDMA'S MAC AND CHEESE

PREHEAT OVEN TO 350° SERVES 6

This recipe comes from my friend Cathy Lorenzo's grandma. Cathy is my dancing friend from New York.

1 lb. ziti or penne rigate
2 10 oz. bars extra-sharp cheddar cheese (I prefer Cracker Barrel brand)
1 stick butter (½ c.)
1½ c. milk
¼ c. Italian bread crumbs
1 shallow 9x13 baking dish

Slice cheese to medium thickness (both bars). Slice butter the same as the cheese. Preheat the oven to 350 degrees.

Boil pasta for 3-4 minutes—you only want to partially cook it. Test by biting one—once you can leave an impression of your teeth, the pasta is done. Ultimately you want the pasta to still be mostly hard so it can absorb the milk, butter, and cheese while baking. Drain and place to the side.

Take the baking dish and place half of the pasta on bottom of dish. Dot with half of the butter squares and cheese squares. Add some of the milk—come up to about the pasta layer or a little bit above (this is a judgment call). Repeat layers once.

Put the dish on a cookie sheet or on top of a piece of aluminum foil to catch any overflow. Bake in preheated oven for 50 minutes.

After 50 minutes, top with Italian bread crumbs, then cook for 10 minutes more. Allow bread crumbs to cook into the top of pasta, which will add extra crunch to the top layer. Serve and enjoy!

PAULA'S TOSSED SALAD

The proportions on this salad are up to you; make it to your tastes and preferences.

mixed greens
chopped green onions
feta cheese
julienned carrot
pine nuts
peeled and finely chopped cucumber
sweet corn kernels

The dressing makes the salad great. It tastes light and is easy to make! This makes more than you will need for the salad, of course, but keep it in the fridge and you can use it later.

1 c. vegetable oil
2/3 c. sugar
1 tsp. pepper
1 tsp. salt
1 clove garlic minced
1 T. fresh lime juice

Shake well and refrigerate to blend flavors. Shake before dressing the salad.

SESSION 07
THE ROAD AHEAD
COMING FROM BEHIND

A FRIEND GAVE ME TWO FREE TICKETS TO SEE THE TENNESSEE TITANS VERSUS THE NEW YORK GIANTS.

IT'S THAT FREE THING THAT ALWAYS SUCKS ME IN. SHE WAS IN TOWN FROM NEW YORK SO IT SEEMED LIKE THE PERFECT OUTING—EXCEPT FOR THE FACT THAT I DON'T LIKE GOING TO LIVE SPORTING EVENTS AND MY FRIEND IS A COWBOYS FAN (TRAITOR THAT SHE IS). ALTHOUGH I'M FANATICAL ABOUT FOOTBALL, I'VE YET TO APPRECIATE THE APPEAL OF ACTUALLY GOING TO GAMES IN PERSON. THE SEATS ARE UNCOMFORTABLE, THE FOOD IS BOTH BAD AND EXPENSIVE, AND I FIND MOST OF THE PEOPLE THERE TO BE ODD. I DON'T THINK THIS IS A JUDGMENT AS MUCH AS A FACT: COSTUMES AND BODY PAINT ARE JUST WEIRD.

As I sat there with my friend, attempting to make out players with our binoculars, I was reminded of yet another reason I would have rather been watching the game at home: you can actually *see* the players when you watch them on television. And as annoying as commercials can be, they don't hold a candle to the guy who was sitting next to me screaming "defense" over and over like he felt bad for the word. I didn't want to say anything, but we didn't have one point on the board and I was kind of thinking we needed something a little more like offense.

At least when you're at home and you're losing this badly you can flip to another channel or go into the kitchen for more Fritos. The things we forgo at live sporting events! I knew it was bad when a moth flew in front of my binoculars and I began to follow it through the stadium. I was intrigued that they could fly as high as the nosebleeds, which grabbed my waning attention from our team who was now losing 21-0 in the fourth quarter. It was time to go. As much as I enjoyed sitting in a hard seat and paying seven dollars for peanuts, I wanted to beat the traffic. My friend obliged.

As we made our way over the walking bridge across the Cumberland River, I couldn't help but glance back at the stadium full of avid fans committed to staying till the bitter end. Those poor, misled souls. Hadn't they heard of cozy living rooms, unlimited chips, and deep couches? Did they

142

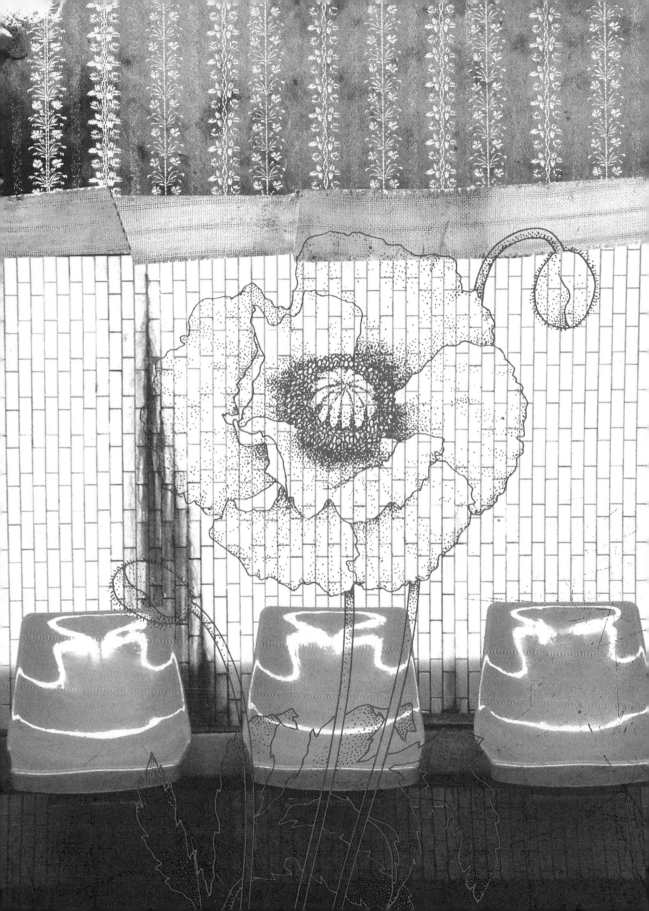

not know of the advent of the remote control? I jumped in the car, gladly shutting the door on a painfully hoodwinked stadium. The din of the engine dulled the screams until we were far enough away to hear absolutely … nothing.

As we drove home in the peaceful quiet, I realized it was still early enough for me to make our evening service at church. I scooted in at the last minute and grabbed a seat on the front row—don't make me pull out my binoculars. My pastor's wife, Kim, got up with her warm and endearing smile and welcomed everyone: "We're so glad you're with us on this chilly evening. We pray you will find warmth for your souls in the midst of worship and community." I was already feeling better. As far as I could tell, no one was dressed up, either. She continued, "We're a little thin tonight, perhaps because I hear the Titans are making a comeback …" I have no idea what Kim said after that. Would it be rude to leave church and drive back to the game? Would this be considered the unpardonable sin? Was I even still worthy of being called a Titans fan? These were the kinds of spiritual questions I was pondering on the front row of church.

After Kim's welcome she sat down beside me as the music began. I turned to her and politely asked in that urgent, whisper-ish, church yell, "Kim, what do you mean the Titans are making a comeback?" "I heard the score is 14-21," she replied. I tried to dismiss the improbable feat while turning my attention to higher things like, well, worship. I comforted myself with the thought that there was no way can they could come back in that short amount of time. By the time the message was over I had all but forgotten about the game. I visited in the sanctuary and watched the coltish kids run around. It was delightful, and I didn't even need a ticket.

After the service I stopped by the home of some friends. Upon walking in the door I was greeted by, "You'll never believe what happened!" Actually … I'm sure I can. The game ended up going down in the annals of sport's history, breaking all kinds of records. It began a 6-0 winning streak for the Titans. And only the crazy committed fans whom I pitied on the way out got to enjoy it. They were loyal and unflinching in their dedication. But mostly, they just stayed. And sometimes that's all that's required. It's just way too easy in life to squirm out of things. We have too many options, rescuers, and remedies for our discomfort. Commitment seems antiquated. Loyalty outdated. When our team is down 21-0, we can call a cab.

I guess I forgot this, but a lot can be said for simply hanging in there. Being in relationship with Jesus is sweet and deeply satisfying on levels we can scarcely describe. It is mysterious and comforting. It is truth. It is life. It is freedom. And it is hard. There are things we can't make sense of. Things that sometimes our idols can explain must better. And even when they can't explain them, they can at least make us feel really good in our confusion. So they constantly call out to us to abandon the path. They remind us of the score and the unlikelihood of a win. Leaving starts to become reasonable.

The past few years have not been easy for me in this regard. Truly by God's power I have been able to dethrone some gods, but since then it hasn't always been bliss along the way. There were exceedingly numerous times when I wanted to go back. Too much seemed stacked against me. Clearly this was a losing battle, and where in the world were the points God was supposed to be putting up on the board? Zero wasn't exactly what I had in mind.

If I can encourage you with silly football analogies and my own real-life pain, I'm telling you straight up—stay. When you're too weary and disillusioned to do anything else, keep staying. God is working out your faith. He's moving in ways you can't even dream of. He's got a comeback plan (though He's never truly behind). So do whatever it takes. If you can't take the guy next to you, wear earplugs. Endure the stale peanuts. Follow the moth. Just don't leave. Hang in there, you. Upsets are especially thrilling.

DAY 01 THE ROAD AHEAD
PATIENCE

Hebrews 11:8
By faith Abraham,
when called to go
to a place he would
later receive as
his inheritance,
obeyed and went,
even though he did
not know where he
was going.

Walking away from our idols is a lifelong process. Though some are miraculously healed from certain addictions or attachments, I am more accustomed to a gradual process. Sometimes we come to moments of godly surrender and decision, but we all have hours, days, and years of walking those decisions out. I want you to feel comfortable in the process, knowing that you can probably expect a squiggly path with successes and failures in your wrestling with idols. This doesn't mean you won't experience huge progress with remarkable deliverance as a result of God's power and your obedience. But it does mean you'll need a few things—patience probably being the first.

Last Sunday I had the profound blessing of being at my home church in Nashville for a Sunday service. I am suddenly aware of how saintly and spiritual this sounds, so let me explain further: it was Sunday brunch at the Village Chapel. Now before I go on, if you happen to have a long history in the western church as we know it, you need to part with your preconceived notions of church potlucks, because brunch at the Village Chapel can heal even the strongest memories of frozen lasagnas and Rice Krispy treats in the fellowship hall.

Brunch at my church is a completely different experience. Waffles, quiche, chocolate croissants, cheese grits with sundried tomatoes—I have a food addiction—doughnuts, custards, blueberry muffins … really, does more need to be said? Well, a little more maybe: on that particular morning the sun blazed through the oversized windows and filled the chapel, leaving only enough room for the sound of instruments and voices, the fragrance of prayer and communion, and echoes of the Word preached. It was a really good day.

As I was getting ready to leave, I ran into a woman I hadn't seen in a long time and barely knew; she had no idea I was writing a Bible study on false gods, making our conversation all the more interesting. She started to tell me that 18 years after laying down her singing and songwriting, she had just begun to pick it up again. She went on to say that music had become a god to her, but also that she tried to defeat it with legalism (hence the dramatic 18-year departure). She continued on, explaining that no one ever told her what was supposed to happen after she laid her idol down. What was to fill the void, if anything? Because she didn't know who or what she was supposed to turn to, she ended up moving onto the next thing—in her case a career in medicine—and ultimately she made a god out of that as well. She further explained that all along she had been looking to find her identity in whatever her career was—it mattered little if it was music or medicine.

Assuming you've been dealing head-on with your own personal pharaohs, you might be at a similar point as my church acquaintance was 18 years ago. What to do now? First, do not be legalistic about the process. Second, I think it helps to know what we can biblically expect.

Sometimes when the Lord calls us to lay something down, He immediately replaces it with a tangible blessing. Other times we are left feeling broken and empty for a seemingly endless season. We wonder what God is doing and whether or not He's still engaged in our lives. It is during these times that we are especially tempted to go running back to the thing that provided us with a false sense of hope and comfort. It is also during these times that we need to rehearse the voice of truth.

What blessings that accompany faith, patience, and persever-ance do each of the following verses describe? (Personally apply the verses to your circumstances, if such a relation exists.)

Psalm 130:5-7   *I wait for the Lord,*

Galatians 6:9   *We shall reap if we faint not.*

Hebrews 6:12   *Faith and patience*

Hebrews 10:35-36   *Endurance*

James 1:3-4   *Testing produces patience*

James 5:7-11   *Resist the devil.*

These verses are incredibly encouraging in that they promise blessings (in due time) when we're obedient. We may not have all the specifics, but we can know that God is going to do some cool stuff in our lives.

Read Genesis 12:1-4 and Hebrews 11:8. What specifics did God give Abraham about where he was going?

God did not provide the details.

Can you think of a time when God asked you to turn from something but wasn't as specific as to what He wanted you to move toward? Briefly write about it below.

Based on these Scripture readings, what do you think God valued as most important in Abraham's journey?
- ❑ Abraham knowing where he was going
- ☒ Abraham being obedient to leave
- ❑ Abraham receiving his blessings
- ❑ Abraham becoming a great nation

Although Abraham didn't know where he was going, list the promises God made that would characterize his journey .

This is just my opinion, but I believe Abraham's obedience was more important than any other detail—even where he was headed. Also note that though some of the details were fuzzy, God's promise of blessings was crystal clear.

No doubt we've all gone through times when we didn't get the whole obedience thing—when we did what the Lord asked us to do and then felt dropped off at the farthest bus stop in the middle of nowhere (my journals are filled with these). Sometimes I have interpreted those times as God's punishment or His condemnation of me. Later I have realized it was just the opposite: He was working out things that were more than I could have hoped for and never could have dreamt up in my finite brain.

Sometimes the Lord immediately replaces what we have left, and other times we are left feeling empty for a time. But I pray that today's readings change how you view the desert times. They are not simply about times of testing and pain, but they promise really good things for us, as we found in each passage. Today—even if the details are blurred—embrace the clarity of promised blessing.

We've all gone through times when we did what the Lord asked us to do and then felt dropped off at the farthest bus stop in the middle of nowhere.

DAY 02 THE ROAD AHEAD
ANTI-LEGALISM

I don't think I've ever heard someone proudly admit to being legalistic. In the thousands of sermons I've listened to and the hundreds of pews I've sat in, I've never heard a pastor say, "We here at such-and-such church are legalistic and are glad you're here this morning."

I find it interesting that though no one claims to be legalistic, most everyone has a list of people or churches they consider legalistic—and those people have their list, who have their list, who have their list … The cycle continues until virtually everyone is accused of it, but no one admits to it. If that is all too complicated, I have a story from kindergarten.

I grew up in a couple of Christian schools where legalism was prevalent, though of course the schools would disagree. I remember being peeled off my mom's neck at the mature age of four on the front stoop of my Christian school. My fun-filled days were comprised mostly of Bible lessons, Scripture-memorization classes, and math. We had coloring breaks, but staying inside the lines was strongly enforced. I'm afraid I grew up to be a rather nervous colorer. My teacher, Mrs. Robertson, walked around with a warm and engaging scowl. Behind her desk, where most people might hang the alphabet in bubble letters with cartoonish bunnies and smiling bears, Mrs. Robertson decided two wooden paddles might be more motivating.

Her plan worked great by the way. I obeyed all the rules. I never talked back and was an excellent student. The only problem was that I would come home—to use my mom's exact terminology—madder than a hornet. As a little kid I would storm in the house and start wreaking havoc on my mom and siblings. After six hours of trying to hold in my wayward tendencies, I would explode. Trying to control my outward behavior without anyone reaching my heart was a losing battle.

I never had a relationship with Mrs. Robertson. I did what she said because I was scared to death of her. Sadly, what she never understood was that her rules could affect my behavior but could never change my heart. Though this isn't an official definition, I think this is pretty much the heart of legalism.

Ezekiel 11:19
I will give them an undivided heart and put a new spirit in them; I will remove from them their heart of stone and give them a heart of flesh.

Write your own definition of legalism.

When people narrow their view of things or take it out of context.

Jesus spoke to the Pharisees about legalism in Matthew 23:25-26. How do these verses tie in to your definition?

The Pharisees had the outward appearance of being clean but their hearts were not.

The Pharisees emphasized the outside. Appearance was the only thing stressed. What was happening in the heart seemed of little consequence to them. Put another way, they were trying to change the inside by outward means.

Read the following verses while looking for the common denominator. Write the shared word in all caps below.

1 Samuel 16:7   2 Chronicles 6:30

2 Chronicles 16:9   Luke 6:45

Heart

In relation to the heart, what verse hit you the most and why?

I Samuel 16:7
the Lord looks at the heart.

These verses aren't suggesting that our heart is the only thing God sees. I think the spirit behind these verses (and many others) is simply this: our outside behavior stems from our heart. We can fake it for a while—sort of like my kindergarten years—but eventually, it all comes out, whether it seeps or explodes. I was mostly an exploder—Lord, have mercy.

Looking back, the thing that bothers me most about my Christian upbringing was the emphasis on behavior and outward appearance. I'm not saying those things aren't important, but I think they take care of themselves when our hearts are right. The problem for me was how in the world was I going to get my heart right? By the middle of high school I was crumbling under the strain of a Christian standard I couldn't maintain. Most of my growing up years I was taught that I had to look and act like a Christian by doing certain things and not doing others. I actually tried very hard and couldn't get it straight. This, yet again, made me madder than a hornet, until I began to understand a truth that I am still unraveling today:

Read Ezekiel 11:19 and 36:26. Very simply, what did God say He would give the Israelites (and, therefore, any believer of the new covenant)? *A new heart & new spirit*

Here's the really crazy thing—go back to the two verses you just read but start one verse earlier (11:18 and 36:25). What, ironically, is removed—or are we cleansed from—when God changes our heart? *Idols*

Could it be any clearer? God deals with our idols when He deals with our hearts. Wow. This is relieving. But it's relieving only because God is the One who changes our hearts. The bottom line is this: we don't have the power in ourselves to dismantle the idols of our hearts. Only by the power and grace of God can such things be accomplished. Moving away from legalism and toward a genuine heart relationship with God will be another important truth to remember on the road ahead.

> **God deals with our idols when He deals with our hearts.**

Write about an area of your life where you have trouble believing this. Where are you still dealing with your "stuff" by either cleaning it up on the outside or trying to change your own heart?

If the "new heart" thing feels too Old Testament to you, we'll close with what I understand to be the New Testament version. Slowly read Romans 7:21-25.

Who is our answer, according to verse 25?
Jesus Christ, my Lord

If this is true, write a prayer in the margin to our Savior in regard to the area of unbelief/struggle you wrote about before. Believe Him for what He's promised—even if the promise of a transformed heart is evolving.

DAY 03 THE ROAD AHEAD
WEAKNESS

2 Corinthians 12:9
My grace is sufficient for you, for my power is made perfect in weakness.

After writing about virtuous things like trust, faith, patience, and perseverance, it may seem odd to throw something like weakness into the mix. But, yes, you will need to be weak for the journey ahead. I just got an e-mail from Alli that ties in pretty well:

I was sitting at home in our tiny apartment listening to a song that always puts my brain in this place where I romanticize everything. I started picturing myself in a movie scene with all the different camera angles spinning around me, sipping a cup of tea while the music plays in the background … and then my husband leaned his head out of the bathroom door …

"Alli, can you come shave the back of my neck for me?"

For a minute I was so frustrated that my movie scene had been interrupted until I had a realization: those are things that make up life. Those in-between moments when I shave the back of my husband's neck are exactly the moments I should be cherishing, not resenting. I realized that if I kept living in my fairy tale world I would end up missing a lot of wonderful things. It was a very selfish place for me to be, mentally. I was believing this lie that my life would be better if music was always playing in the background, if it was more "romantic." But in fact, since I stopped idolizing that mindset, that fairy tale, I've started seeing more beauty in my everyday life than I knew was there.

His eyes are not running across the earth looking for the woman who lives in a romantic movie set of perfection. He is looking for the real, the weak, and the one who concedes need for Him.

God shows up in our reality. He shows up in our weakness. His eyes are not running across the earth looking for the woman who lives in a romantic movie set of perfection. He is looking for the real, the weak, and the one who concedes need for Him. And how thankful I am, for there are so many areas of my life that are extremely weak, areas I wish I had better control over.

Just yesterday I decided that the road and its buffet of eclectic cuisine had not only shoved itself into my body in the form of fat cells, but had also begun to dominate me. So I decided I was going to start eating a little less and a little healthier. Time to reel it in, I mused.

152

Day one: for breakfast, a granola bar; for lunch, a Greek salad; for dinner, shrimp over jalapeño cheese grits, artichoke with brie dip, crab cakes, pita slices with mozzarella chunks, molten lava chocolate cake with homemade Oreo ice cream. Day two: leftover Snickers cheesecake and a glass of whole milk. It's only 11:27 in the morning, so this is as far as I've gotten on my diet. Weakness, my greatest downfall. Or is it?

Now the whole dieting thing is halfway tongue in cheek (albeit one hundred percent true), but my point is that we are human, thus we are weak. No matter how disciplined a person may be, she will have weaknesses in her life. Sometimes the discipline itself is to compensate for or cover up a weakness. And weakness doesn't always mean that we lack discipline or fortitude. It can mean a thousand other things as well—we're unkind to our family members, we gossip, we can't say no to alcohol, we're jealous. Or they can be things that have nothing to do with sin issues: physical ailments, mental challenges, financial hardships, relational strains. Weakness is all-inclusive. It inhabits our flesh. But can weakness be one of our sweetest gifts? I think so.

Read 2 Corinthians 12:1-10.

A little background might be helpful. Most commentators emphatically believe Paul is speaking of himself when he talks about knowing a certain "man" in verse 2. When he writes about being caught up into the third heaven, Paul is referring to the throne room of God. He is also explaining that the vision was so vivid he couldn't tell if it physically happened to him, if he saw it all in his mind, or if perhaps heaven was brought down to him. He doesn't make it clear, and most commentators don't pretend to know. Either way, these are just a few details that hopefully bring a little more clarity to the reading.

In verse 5, what is the only thing Paul says he will boast about?

Infirmaties

Why did God allow Satan to send a thorn in Paul's flesh?

To show Paul that God's grace is sufficient.

Why do you think Paul didn't tell us what his thorn in the flesh was?

To show us he was not perfect.

Verse 8 says that Paul pleaded with the Lord three times to take it away. What does this tell you about prayer? (Write honestly, not what you think the "right" answer is.)

Paul's thorn in the flesh is said to have been a messenger of Satan. I have always found this a little perplexing until recently. Not that I have a full handle on it, but I believe the Lord has revealed some of what this means as a result of some experiences in my own life. I have had some deeply painful losses at the hand of some unjust people. I remember questioning God, begging him to restore what was lost to me. After many months (sometimes even years), I began to see that what some people meant to cause me harm, God was able to use for good. Matthew Henry's commentary puts it this way: "This thorn in the flesh is said to be a messenger of Satan which he sent for evil; but God designed it, and overruled it for good."[1]

Another example of this in the Old Testament has to do with Joseph and the brothers who sold him into slavery. How is Genesis 50:20 similar to 2 Corinthians 12:7?

God used to bring about something else

Can you think of a time in your life when God used something that was intended for harm to bring about good? Briefly write about it below.

I have sought many of my false gods because of my weaknesses. I think this would be true for all of us. If you think back to some of the personal pharaohs you listed in the first week of this study, you probably see that a certain weakness drove you there. That is when the reality of having weaknesses betrays us. But when we turn to God in our weaknesses, we find what Paul found in verses 9-10.

What came as a result of Paul not only embracing his thorn but also boasting in it? (See vv. 9-10.)

Paul became stronger in the Lord

I hope that today's writings allow you to relax a bit. I'd like to remove a little pressure and have you walk away encouraged. You might think me a tad optimistic considering we've just read about messengers of

Satan, thorns in people's flesh, and prayers that aren't answered to our specifications. But verse 10 contains the incredibly encouraging part, "For when I am weak, then I am strong." It is encouraging because I am weak. I have profound weaknesses—some of them are prone to temptation, others are physical, and perhaps have even been sent my way by Satan. But not without God's sovereign hand over every dart, thorn, and ailment. Not without His grace being completely sufficient for me in every trial I face.

God knows we are but flesh. Even the Apostle Paul was flesh-bound. In the preceding chapter (11:29-30) he says, "Who is weak, and I am not weak?" He goes on to say, "If I must boast, I will boast of the things that show my weakness." So his weaknesses can be exalted? No. That would be to totally miss the point, to exalt victimization. Paul boasted in his weaknesses because he knew that God's grace and power would rest on those areas, exalting God's strength, not Paul's.

Today I encourage you to embrace your weakness. View it in a new light. From a different angle. See your weaknesses and struggles as opportunities to reveal God's power and grace in your life.

> See your weaknesses and struggles as opportunities to reveal God's power and grace.

Write about a particular weakness in your life and how God's strength could be made perfect in it. I would also encourage dialoguing with God about this area, knowing that His grace is sufficient.

DAY 04 THE ROAD AHEAD
TRUST

Psalm 121:1-2
I lift up my eyes to
the hills—where
does my help come
from? My help
comes from the
LORD, the Maker of
heaven and earth.

I think, ultimately, our dependence on our functional gods is primarily a matter of trust; we don't trust God, while we do trust our idols to bring us what we want and need.

I'm right in the middle of a potentially life-changing trust issue now. I've unexpectedly hit a fork in my otherwise smooth road, and am faced with an opportunity that could move me hundreds of miles away from my home—the home that I love, the home that's surrounded by deep friendships, the home in which I've finally begun to settle … Not to mention the parks, restaurants, and southern accents. *Don't make me go!*

Through the cacophony of a little panic and a lot of angst, I keep hearing the word *trust*. Not the word *surrender* (that was back in week 3, I think) because, to the best of my ability I have surrendered. I will go where the Lord wants me to go. But I'm finding that trust can be entirely different, though the two often overlap. One of my friends recently said surrender is about the will; trust is about the heart. I am having a hard time trusting God as I explore something that would mean giving up so much of what I deeply love and depend on.

I believe God wants my trust, since trust speaks deeply of relationship.

I would just as soon pick a different topic altogether, take a sleeping pill, and crawl under my covers—never mind that it's 3:44 in the afternoon (denial can be such a good thing). But I believe God wants my trust, since trust speaks deeply of relationship. It is a rare moment we trust someone on a heart level with whom we're not in relationship. So that's where I am—working through yet another layer in my relationship with God, prayerful that I will come out on the other side as one who trusts Him more deeply.

Do you obey God while not relating to Him? Have you surrendered to Him while not trusting Him? Do you feel especially intimate with Him? Briefly describe where you're at.

Perhaps this is all still a bit confusing. It's possible that a little Jonah might clear things up. Keep in mind that God had told Jonah to go preach in Ninevah, but Jonah responded by fleeing on a ship to Tarshish and was eventually thrown overboard. The story picks up there.

Read Jonah 1:17–3:3.

Look at 3:1-3 again. What does it say Jonah did in response to God's second command to go to Ninevah?

Jonah ___obeyed___ the word of the Lord and went to Ninevah.

Continue on in the story reading 3:4-10. What was the result of Jonah's obedience? *The people turned to God*

I'm intrigued that the Book of Jonah doesn't end here. For the sake of happy endings, it could say: God tells man to obey, man refuses, God disciplines man, man obeys, God blesses man, the end. Too bad the story had to be realistic. Enter chapter 4, which is rather unflattering to Jonah, revealing a heart issue that remained undetected even in Jonah's obedience.

Read 4:1-3. What is revealed about Jonah in these verses?
He got angry and wanted to die.

Based on this story, is it possible to be obedient (to surrender to God's commands) while not trusting God's heart?
☑ yes ☐ no

I have a feisty little cousin who, as a little girl, was constantly bucking the system. One day her Aunt Heather took her shopping, and she got miffed about something or another. Heather made her sit down on a bench in the store. With arms crossed, she said, "I'm sitting down on the outside, but in my heart I'm standing up." I'm sure this isn't good, but I have to say I kinda love my cousin for stuff like this, 'cause doesn't a little Jonah exists in all of us?

On the outside Jonah was preaching in Ninevah, but perhaps in his heart he was still on a ship to Tarshish. Isn't it interesting that in the midst of his obedience—or his ultimate surrender to God's direction—we find a man who is so mad at God he wants to die? I think the bottom line for Jonah was obedience without heart, surrender without trust.

I believe God wants both from us. I know in my own situation He desires me to enter into deeper relationship with Him. He is calling me not merely to seek an answer *from* Him (should I take this opportunity or not?), but to seek an answer *with* Him. To trust Him during the process of exploring His heart for my life's decisions, not just to throw my hands up in resignation, sighing, *Thy will be done!*

Let me add, I would hate for anyone to think that trusting and feeling are necessarily the same things. Many times I have simply clenched my teeth and chosen obedience, trusting His commands but not "feeling the love" on any level. I know my mom is currently in that situation. She feels very strongly that the Lord has asked her to serve some specific people. She's doing it out of obedience, but she's not quite feeling it yet.

Both scripturally and experientially, obedience without warm, tingly feelings will always be some part of our faith journey—and definitely nothing to feel bad about. But even that is quite different than what I understand Jonah's situation to have been. He was obeying while his heart disagreed with the heart of God. He preached repentance and mercy to the Ninevites while his heart wanted judgment on them. Right now my mom isn't necessarily feeling excited about what God has asked her to do, but she agrees with God's heart in the matter. As I continue to seek God's heart, I am attempting to look at the bigger picture, not just the smaller answer. Psalm 121 offers encouragement to me as I look at God's intimate involvement in our lives.

> **Meditate on Psalm 121. Let the details penetrate.**
>
> **Regarding trust, what speaks most deeply to you out of this psalm? Describe the passage and how it affects you. Push through to trust the God who today is our shade.**

2. My help comes from the Lord,

Obedience without warm, tingly feelings will always be some part of our faith journey.

DAY 05 THE ROAD AHEAD
PRAYER

I don't know if you're like me, but it's far easier for me to sit and read my Bible than to pray. People who can spend hours in prayer always intrigue me. One of my friends has a mother who has spent years in intercessory prayer. Every time she comes to visit I ask her a million questions about her ministry, how she hears from the Lord, what new amazing stories she has, and how she prays. I so desire a deeper prayer life, but it hasn't been the easiest thing to come by. One thing I am currently learning is that praying is something I simply have to choose to do.

A few years ago I was in the throes of a painful situation from which I couldn't seem to get released. I had done hours on hours of Bible study. I sought wise advice from counselors and friends. Still, nothing seemed to change. I saw things more clearly and even understood things about myself and the situation, but nothing lifted. As the pressure mounted, I felt increasingly hopeless. One morning I called my mom—a strong woman of prayer—and asked her to pray with me regularly about what I was going through. I realized that prayer was my only answer.

> **Read Matthew 17:14-22 and Mark 9:14-31.**
> **Why couldn't the disciples drive out the evil spirit from the boy?**

They did not pray.

If the disciples couldn't heal apart from prayer, I'm figuring it's safe to surmise that we can't either. Regardless of what we're fighting, prayer is an essential element we can't survive without. When it comes to the road ahead, we can only walk forward in prayer.

Today our reading was short, because I want us to spend as much time as we can allow in prayer. One thing that my friend's mom always tells me is to pray God's Word. She has said to me, "The Bible is God's manifest will—we know this to be true. Since we have His will in front of us, let's pray that will, knowing that He hears and responds."

I encourage you to flip through the psalms, or perhaps some of Paul's letters, and find some passages that particularly minister to you. Find promises and truths that you desire to cling to. When you come across those verses, pray them back to God. If you prefer to write your prayer, do so in the margin.

Mark 9:24, HCSB
Immediately the father of the boy cried out, "I do believe! Help my unbelief."

1. Matthew Henry, *Matthew Henry's Concise Commentary on the Whole Bible* (Nashville: Thomas Nelson, 1997), 1131.

CHICKEN CUTLETS
PREHEAT OVEN TO 350° SERVES 6

I call this "Cathy Lorenzo's Authentic Italian, Ridiculous, Over-the-Top, Will-Make-You-Cry Chicken Cutlets."

1 lb. boneless, skinless chicken cutlets, cut in half and pounded thin
3 eggs
Italian bread crumbs
canola oil
8 oz. block of mozzarella cheese
1 lb. any kind of pasta

Add canola oil to a deep frying pan. Put enough in to cover the cutlets when placed in the oil. Heat oil on low flame and be careful, as the oil will pop. While oil is heating, place breadcrumbs in a bowl and beat the eggs in a separate bowl. Take each cutlet and place in the egg, fully covering both sides. Then place in breadcrumbs, fully covering both sides. Once cutlets are covered in egg and breadcrumbs, place a couple of pieces into the hot oil and allow each side to brown. Watching them closely, cook until done and then place them onto dish with a paper towel underneath them to absorb excess oil.

Continue the above steps until all the chicken is cooked. Preheat oven to 350 degrees.

Slice mozzarella cheese to a medium thickness and set aside. Have a baking dish ready. Place a good amount of "mom's sauce" (see next page) on the bottom of dish. Add as many cutlets as you can. Add more sauce to top of cutlets and place the sliced mozzarella cheese on top.

Place into the preheated oven (have tin foil under dish for any spills). Cook for only 15-20 minutes, since the chicken has already been cooked thoroughly. Mainly just allow the cheese to melt and the sauce to cook a bit into the chicken. Place on table with a side of pasta. Don't forget the Italian bread and butter!

MOM'S SAUCE

(a.k.a., Cathy Lorenzo's Mom's Authentic Italian, Ridiculous, Over-the-Top, Will-Make-You-Cry Sauce)

2 28 oz. cans of tomato puree
2 bulbs fresh garlic, minced (yes bulbs, not just cloves)
assortment of meats (spare ribs, pork necks, sausage, beef)
fresh basil (4-5 leaves cut into small pieces)
1 bay leaf
dried oregano
dried parsley
olive oil

Coat the bottom of a large pot with olive oil. Use enough so the meat doesn't stick to the pan. Place meat in hot oil. Sautee until meat is browned on all sides (meat does not have to be cooked throughout, just browned on the outside). Once browned, pour in the cans of tomato puree and add ½ can of water from each can. Add fresh garlic and fresh basil. (Cathy's mom always said, "If you think you have enough garlic, add more!") Add bay leaf and dried oregano and parsley to taste. The more the better for me. Add salt and pepper to taste as well.

Cover the pot. Cook on low heat for 3-4 hours (or longer; the longer it cooks, the richer the flavor). Allow the sauce to darken and the meat to cook thoroughly through—meat will begin to fall off the bone, which is a good thing.

Once you feel the sauce is done to your liking, pull all meat and bones out of the sauce. Set aside. (Mom usually placed the sausage and spare ribs on the table for all who wanted to eat them—the necks were usually stripped off the meat and thrown away—whatever you like!) Discard bay leaf and serve with chicken cutlets and pasta.

SESSION 08
MAKING ROOM
CLEANING THE HEART

THE FOLLOWING POPPED INTO MY E-MAIL THIS EVENING AND I COULDN'T KEEP IT TO MYSELF. IT'S FROM A DEAR FRIEND WHO IS UPDATING ME ON A BIT OF HER LIFE. IT HAPPENED TO FIT THE "MAKING ROOM" THEME, SO I HAD TO SHARE IT . . .

I am sitting on my bed, in my new house, listening to a song about a broken spirit and a contrite heart. I have found the beauty in being broken and repenting of the places I have not allowed the Lord to "overflow." I am guilty of finding my own ways to fill my void, to give me a sense of hope. But hope deferred makes the heart sick. Oh, how the things I've placed my faith in besides the Lord have failed me and brought about such sickness. I have finally come to a place of surrender. To God be the glory. My prayer is to always remember this time of life and the tender closing of our study together about having no other gods above our God.

My husband and I recently bought our first home together. We have been married one year and have lived in the same apartment since we married. The last few weeks have been filled with endless days of renovating our new house while we still lived in our apartment. We redid the floors, painted, and tried to make the house our own. It seemed like every time our contractor went to "fix" something, it unveiled three more things that needed to be fixed. Sound familiar? Oh, how much this represents the renovation my heart has been under these last few years.

On one end of our move we had a house undergoing renovation. On the other end, we were packing and preparing to start living in our new home. Some friends came over and helped me pack my kitchen. I don't like to ask for help so this was especially a blessing. It's also pretty symbolic of how much we need to lean on those the Lord has placed in our lives. Sometimes you need a friend to say, "You need to get rid of this brown sugar; it's as hard as a rock!"

Well, some other things needed to go from our old apartment. Things a little more profound than brown sugar. As I packed my box of memorabilia I found a ton of letters from a boyfriend from high school and my first years of college. He was the first guy I gave my heart to and really loved. Because I was with him during some very tumultuous times, my relationship with him gave me

a sense of security. I kept hanging on to the hope that one day the things that needed to be fixed about our relationship would finally work themselves out. In a way, I have always felt like that relationship didn't end with much closure. Though I knew we weren't right for each other, I still loved him and his family very much. Eventually I met my husband, fell in love, and got married.

I came to find out, however, that just because you get married, those ties are not immediately removed from your heart. For so many years, even before I got married, I asked God to take those ties from me. I grew bitter toward the Lord over time for not breaking them. However, when I found the cards, letters, printed e-mails, etc. I was saving, I realized that I had really never surrendered those ties to the Lord. He did not rip them out of my hands … He waited for me to repent and hand them over. Oh, how I thought I had done that so many times. Why, then, were these "symbols" of our relationship still in my memory box and so important to me?

Two days before we moved into our new home, I stacked the letters into a pile, lit a candle, and cried. I grieved this loss and allowed myself to feel the pain of what that relationship meant to me, and of the loss I experienced when it ended. I became painfully aware of the hope I tried to suck out of each of the letters. Hope that always came up short. As I sat there reminiscing over the pile, I came across one note that I thought I would hold back. Before I knew it, the note I was holding accidentally caught fire on the candle I had lit. I tore out of the house in my bathrobe, ashes following after me, and stood outside in the cold as I watched half of it burn. I then knew what I had to do.

I gathered up all my notes and memories, put them in a bamboo box, and tied it with a ribbon. These memories were special to me; they were a huge part of my life. I could not just throw them in a dumpster. I care deeply for this guy and his family. That's just the bottom line, and though I've tried for years to feel some other way, the Lord assured me that it is okay to recognize those profound feelings … and then give them to Him so I can move on. And so I did …

I set the bamboo box in our fireplace and had myself a last long and good cry. I can just imagine as the smoke billowed out of the fireplace what an offering that was to my Jesus. Jesus has captivated my heart. He has poured out such love to me. I am full … but before that moment there was part of my heart I hadn't fully surrendered. He couldn't fit into that part of my heart because something else was taking up space. I love my husband so much. I don't want some-

thing like this taking up room in my heart that should belong to him (the Lord leases him this part of my heart, you see). My commitment to the Lord and to my husband was honored as I said goodbye to the false sense of security and hope that these notes offered me. And I emphasize the word false.

I know my marriage will benefit from my surrender, as will the children that we have together one day. I have greatly benefited even in this short time. I feel freed up. Those ties that I was holding onto are no longer mine. I have given them to the Lord and allowed Him to fill that space. Before, I was afraid that if I did away with those letters, that part of my life would be gone and therefore leave a huge, gaping hole. However, now I know that, instead, Jesus has made a home there. He has redeemed the pain, and He has consumed the joy that did live there at one time. Now when I look back at that period of my life, I see Jesus. And more important, when I look ahead to my future, I see Jesus. When I sit in the peace of my present, I see Jesus. In my relationship with my husband, in our new house, in the new memories we are making, I see Jesus. Beauty has sprung from the ashes. Praise be to the Living God. Capital "G."

DAY 01 MAKING ROOM
SOMETIMES ALONE

Daniel 3:16
Shadrach, Meshach
and Abednego
replied to the king,
"O Nebuchadnez-
zar, we do not need
to defend our-
selves before you
in this matter."

Making room is why we have been turning from our false gods. It's the ambition of our hard and sometimes painful work, as my friend so beautifully portrayed. It is the hope we are holding out for. At least it's the hope I'm holding out for. I think my heart would just stop beating if I didn't have the belief that as I clear out the lesser idols I am making space for the Living God. Many people have made room for God in stunning measures, stood back, and watched Him overflow the space. You or I cannot be the exception.

When I bought my condo a couple years ago, so many things needed to be changed and renovated, I had no idea where to start. When my good friend Tonia came to visit, she was a lot clearer on the matter. I remember it was close to midnight when she emerged from the bathroom imploring me to start there. She did have a point: it boasted the original gold tile from the 70s, which for some reason encouraged a previous owner to "decorate" with rose bush stencils around the ceiling and vanity. I think her goal was to create something even more hideous than the tile, perhaps to create a diversion. It was a valiant effort.

I don't know if you've been in a similar predicament, but bathroom renovations aren't cheap, which is why Tonia sincerely suggested I subsist off cans of black beans until I saved enough money to re-do the room (this took two years).

Last month I was pleased to call Tonia with the details as my favorite handyman took a sledgehammer to the tub, vanity, mirror, and tile. It was a glorious process. I think I heard the Hallelujah Chorus from on high when the toilet was removed. By day's end, everything had been taken back to the studs. It was a clean slate, a fresh palette for something I had long been wanting. The newly-emptied space became a reminder to me: I couldn't bring in the new without first removing the old.

PERSONAL REFLECTION: Since we began our study together, in what area(s) of your life have you begun creating room for God by removing idols?

Has the process left any empty spaces of loneliness?

Just this morning a friend gave me a verse from Jeremiah: "I sat alone because your hand was on me" (Jer. 15:17). I have been struggling with loneliness as a result of some decisions I've made to separate myself from things I don't feel comfortable with anymore. This means giving up some "people time," which I greatly value.

I'm by no means advocating a pious disconnect from friends who don't hold our same beliefs—we are to be right in the middle of our worlds, loving and sharing the redemption of Christ. But sometimes God calls us to remove ourselves from certain settings or gatherings that compromise the road God has convinced us to walk.

I remember when Lauri left her "dream job" due to her own heart's convictions. She had worked hard in the make-up industry and had finally achieved status in a recognizable outfit. Things were going well for her career-wise, but on a heart level she described herself getting pulled into areas she didn't want to go. She said, "I desired to fit in but eventually realized that by 'fitting in' I began to lose who I was. There was a lot of gossip and an over-focus on materialism. I could feel myself getting lured in. It finally occurred to me that it was okay if I didn't fit in. As a matter of fact, I realized I didn't want to fit in. Eventually, God allowed me to quit the store and work solely from home. I still love the make-up industry and get to freelance a lot. Sometimes I struggle with the thought that who I am is defined by what I do. But I never wonder if giving up my 'ideal' job for the sake of following God was really worth it. God has blessed me too much to think otherwise."

Today we're going to look at a few biblical characters who stood alone to make room for God. I pray their stories will encourage you as we continue, even if we have to fly solo for a time.

> **Speaking of people who have turned from idols and made room, turn to Daniel chapter 3 and read the chapter in its entirety. Be looking for ways that Shadrach, Meschach, and Abednego made room for God by not bowing down to an idol. By the way, from here on I will lovingly refer to these three as SM&A (too much space taken up otherwise—save the trees!).**

> Sometimes God calls us to remove ourselves from certain settings or gatherings that compromise the road God has convinced us to walk.

What was the consequence for not bowing to the statue?
❑ imprisonment ☒ incineration ❑ loss of position

How many others besides SM&A refused to bow down?
Daniel

What do verses 13 and 19 say about Nebuchadnezzar's temperament?
He was furious

Has another person's anger ever made you afraid to stand on your convictions? If so, describe.

I never really thought about it too much until today, but SM&A were ultimately alone in this. Their decision separated them from the rest of the officials. Not to mention, they had to do it in the face of great anger.

This is a good reminder for me as I'm a quintessential people-pleaser. I hate the idea of being divided from those around me, especially people I love. I get crazy over the phrase "let's agree to disagree." To me, that's the ultimate blow in a discussion. I know this is impossible—and not even healthy—but when it comes to the people I love, I want to always agree to agree. As a result, it feels especially difficult for me when I have to separate myself due to the convictions the Lord has put in my heart. If I were SM&A, I wouldn't have wanted to bow down, but I would have wanted to smooth the whole thing over—make sure Neb's feelings weren't hurt, and make sure all the other officials understood where I was coming from. Which brings me to my next note …

Read verses 15-16 and describe SM&A's response to the king. How did they defend themselves?
They said they would not bow down and their God would deliver them from the fire, and if not they still would not bow

Also read verse 16 in the King James Version: "Shadrach, Meshach, and Abednego, answered and said to the king, O Nebuchadnezzar, we are not *careful* to answer thee in this matter" (italics mine). The word *careful* here means hasty, to have need of, ready. It implies a sense of urgency and eagerness. In essence they were saying, "We are NOT urgent, eager, or needful to answer or defend ourselves."

Given the urgency of the situation—being thrown into a furnace—how do you explain their non-urgent response?

They believed God would help them.

When we refuse to bow our hearts to the functional gods in our lives, we inevitably become separate from them, and sometimes from others. The time-lapse between the emptiness and God's filling can sometimes create spaces of anxiety, fear, and questioning that can lure us back to our idols. The space can also spawn urgency, hastiness, and a false need to overly explain ourselves to others. Sometimes I fight an overwhelming need to explain my decisions when really the best thing to do is simply rest quietly in my convictions with the Lord. Sometimes the best response is a peaceful, humble non-response.

According to verses 16-18, what do you think was behind their noticeably calm and controlled behavior?

Faith and trust in God

I would love to know what you wrote to the preceding question. As I've pondered it in my own heart, I have to think they had a great deal of confidence and trust in the Lord. I don't think this was something they simply came up with in the moment. I believe this speaks of years of daily trust in God and subsequent obedience to Him. It speaks of a deep belief that had grown over time. They knew God was big enough to deliver them—however that looked—and they didn't feel the urge to try to work that out themselves. Of course, this is not to say that if you are a new follower of Christ, He won't give you that same strength and resolve He gave to them. Scripture tells us that He uses trials and hardships to grow our faith, so no matter how long or little you've known the Lord, He will give you all you need (Jas. 1:1-5).

In closing today, I want to highlight the last statement in verse 29 (NIV). Fill in the three blanks: "... for _no other God_ **can deliver in this way."**

PERSONAL REFLECTION: How does this verse encourage you to make room for God by not giving your heart to false gods?

This morning I praise Him. I praise Him. I praise Him. No other god can deliver in this way. Thank you, Jesus. No other god can fill the empty space in our lives like our God. Rest in Him today. Make no defense. Refrain from hasty explanations. Be still and know that He is God.

> Sometimes I fight an overwhelming need to explain my decisions when really the best thing to do is simply rest quietly in my convictions with the Lord.

DAY 02 MAKING ROOM
FAITH

Hebrews 11:1
Now faith is being
sure of what we hope
for and certain of
what we do not see.

Sometimes not bowing to our idols can mean standing alone for a time. I struggle with this because little distresses me more than being alone. So it takes great faith when I have to make decisions for God that cause loneliness. I have to continually remind myself (as I did this morning) of the promises in Scripture. How God blesses those who wait on Him. How He answers the Hannahs and Ruths and Esthers of Scripture. How He is near to the brokenhearted. If I lose my faith in Him, I will invariably return to the gods I have left behind.

Thankfully, my nogs get this. Carrie and her husband have especially had to walk this thing out. They've taken some huge faith steps related to having kids, job changes, and house changes. I've never seen so much up in the air for any child-expecting couple. Carrie, it's all yours…

I am so excited that you're all to this chapter! While I was going through the other seven chapters with the nogs, we each had our own revelations and momentous times of seeing God fill the spaces we were clearing out in our lives. This entire year I felt like my husband and I had to clear out the stronghold of decisions based on what others thought instead of going where God wanted us to go. This year, we made a lot of changes in both our lives and careers that probably seemed too risky to some, and too overwhelming to others, and I'm sure we left some people wondering why in the world we would put ourselves in such a vulnerable and stressful place. We really value the opinion of our parents, other family, and friends, but these decisions needed to be strictly based on God's leading.

It hasn't always been easy, but we have seen God do miraculous things in each area that we allowed Him to fill in our lives. It's all been about faith. Because we trusted Him, He gave us the grace to walk through it even when we thought we weren't going to make it. Not only did we get to see this firsthand to increase our faith, but the people surrounding us also got to see each blessing was coming from God alone.

*We were obedient so He could do the miraculous. We've got
a child on the way, a new home, and a brand-new business.
None of this happened overnight, but it's all been about faith;
and every bit's been worth it.*

**Read Hebrews 11:1-40 as slowly and thoughtfully as you can.
You may have read this passage many times; if so, pray that
God will show you something new in this reading. Then write
verbatim a verse or verses that stood out to you.**

*Hebrews 11:6
"But without faith it is impossible to please
Him, for he who comes to God must believe that
He is, and that He is a rewarder of those who
diligently seek Him."*

**Name some things the different people mentioned were look-
ing forward to. In essence, what were their future hellos?**

Heaven, the city of God.

Hebrews 11:15 is one of the most meaningful verses to me in all
Scripture, because it shows God realizes how hard leaving can be.
Whether we're leaving a physical landscape full of memories, moving
from loved relationships, or turning our backs on some coveted sin,
leaving can be hard. Which is why this verse tells us if we dwell on all
we've left behind, we will be tempted to return. I think this is what
happened to the Israelites in the wilderness: they filled their minds with
the things of Egypt and didn't dwell on the promises of Canaan God
gave them. They had it all reversed.

> If they had been
> thinking of the country
> they had left, they
> would have had oppor-
> tunity to return
> (Heb. 11:15).
>
> Truly, if they had
> been mindful of that
> country from whence
> they came out, they
> might have had
> opportunity to
> have returned
> (Heb. 11:15, KJV).

I well relate; this verse jumped out at me a number of years ago when I
felt the Lord moving me on from a particular place. It wasn't a physical
setting; it was an emotional place—a heart attachment that I needed
to let go of. As I moved forward with grief and loss, I found that what
I occupied my mind with had a profound effect on me. My mind
constantly drifted back. I had to grab it and fill it with other thoughts
as the vibrant memories from before fought to hang on. Eventually He
replaced the old with the new.

End today by describing something you want to say hello to in your life, something you want to greet, even if you're a bit timid about it. Just like the people mentioned in Hebrews, write down where your faith will be tested in greeting this new thing.

We've looked at so much Scripture this week already. We've seen how God has blessed those who made room for Him. On a personal note, I just want to share how deeply the Lord has been blessing me in ways so specific to Him and me. He knows my path. He knows the decisions I've had to make. He has walked me through the clearing out process. For the moment, He's filling in the spaces in ways that are blowing me away. If I can leave you with one thought today, it's this: <u>whatever God is urging you to clear away cannot begin to be compared to what He ultimately wants to bring you.</u> (I think I heard Beth Moore speak that sentence several months ago. At the time I heard it, it was a concept I believed; now it is a truth I am living.) God, you are so good.

DAY 03 MAKING ROOM
THE PROMISED LAND

If it takes faith to says goodbye, it takes faith to say hello. The real travesty is going through all the pain of a goodbye but never enjoying the fulfillment of a new hello. The Israelites left Egypt but hadn't replaced it with Canaan. In between lay heat, sand, and manna, which weren't all bad. After all, every follower of Christ will have to walk through the desert at times in life—it is the bridge between the old and the new. But the idea is to go through the desert, not to attach there, and that takes faith.

I remember being in Christian school as a kid, rehearsing all the things we weren't supposed to do: no lying, no cheating, no talking back, no chewing gum in class (is this a verse?). But I rarely remember hearing about the good things to replace the things we were to leave behind. This has somewhat carried into adulthood for me. I know what I'm supposed to turn from, but I don't always carry it full circle. Leaving our idols is not the final goal. We leave them so we can experience the fullness of Christ, who is our life! Don't miss today's verse: "He brought us out … to bring us in." We make room for God to fill it. We say goodbye to say hello. Today we'll see that faith played out in the lives of the Israelites as they cross the Jordan to enter the promised land.

> **Deuteronomy 6:23**
> He brought us out from there to bring us in and give us the land that he promised on oath to our forefathers.

Read Deuteronomy 8:6-18, a description of the desert and the promised land. As you read, list a few characteristics of each.

The Desert	The Promised Land
Dry, hot, snakes, scorpions, lot of sand.	Good land, brooks of water, fountains & springs, Wheat & barley, vines & fig trees, pomegranates, olive oil, honey, iron ore, copper, herds & flocks multiply, beautiful houses

I love the clarity of this passage. The desert had snakes and scorpions. The promised land came with oil and pools of water. But the Lord was their Provider in both places, and He didn't want them to forget that.

Looking at verse 17, why was God concerned that they might forget Him in the good land?

They thought their power & might of their hand gained them the wealth.

Of what does He remind them in verse 18?

God gives us the power to get wealth.

I need to be reminded that God is the One who gives the ability to produce and increase wealth. Any talent, strength, or skill is a gift from Him, and the blessings that come as a result are also His gifts.

Have you been using a skill or talent that you have forgotten was a unique gift from God? If so, explain …

We've gotten a good glimpse of what the promised land is going to look like for the Israelites. Let's now look at a bit of their journey.

Read Joshua chapters 3 and 4. I want you to get the full sense of their journey.

I love 3:5—"Tomorrow the Lord will do amazing things among you." My spirit is convinced that these are the things we have to look forward to when we, by faith, move from the idols of our hearts.

> My spirit is convinced that we have "amazing things" to look forward to when we, by faith, move from the idols of our hearts.

Last week the girls and I shared very intently about the things we were withholding from the Lord. I loved the honesty, because relinquishment can feel very scary at first. For most of us, the things we were holding back from God were our relationships, family, careers, and futures. These were the premium entities we wanted to control. But as we release our idols from the clutches of our hearts, I believe the Lord cheers, saying, "Now I can do amazing things. I'm ready to take you to the other side." The question often is, do we want to go?

After forty years of desert wanderings, the Israelites were ready to go. Sometimes it takes that long to get so sick of doing life our way for us to become open for change. I am too often like the New Orleans guy who wants to stay put at all costs. Sometimes saying hello scares me.

174

PERSONAL REFLECTION: Are you open to the Lord doing amazing things in your life? Are you open for change? Are you open for new hellos? The questions all overlap, but one might strike you more than another. Write your response below.

I want to tie things up with two closing thoughts: First, verses 4:12-13 indicate that 40,000 armed men crossed over in front of the Israelites for battle. I thought it was interesting that even the promised land would require a fight. On the other side of that, I was blessed to see that the Lord had sent all of these soldiers ahead of the Israelites for protection, and had instructed the priests to cross over last. The people were hemmed in on both sides. It's a beautiful picture of God's divine covering in our lives.

Second, read Joshua 5:11-12. Let verse 12 sink in: "The manna stopped the day after they ate this food from the land; there was no longer any manna for the Israelites, but that year they ate of the produce of Canaan."

The Lord will not allow us to be in the desert forever. Manna is only for a season. If you are going through a lean time of wafers on your tongue and burning sand beneath your feet, this too shall pass.

Once the Israelites ate the milk and honey of Canaan, the manna ceased. Isn't it interesting that it didn't cease before they ate of the land? I think there's something here for us: they had to eat the fruit before the old would melt away.

Take hold of the blessings God has put in front of you.

> The Lord will not allow us to be in the desert forever. Manna is only for a season.

DAY 04 MAKING ROOM
PERSEVERANCE

Ruth 1:16
Where you go I will go, and where you stay I will stay. Your people will be my people and your God my God.

I'd love to dig deeper into each of the stories we've looked at this week, but I'm hoping that even these brief sketches will speak deeply to your own journey. Today and tomorrow we'll be looking at the person of Ruth. We 'll only scratch the surface of the book, but hopefully the pieces will encourage you to keep making room. Today we'll look at the bold choices she made, and tomorrow we'll focus on how those choices made room for God to act in her life and in the lives of generations to come.

Read Ruth 1:1-22.
Where did Naomi and her husband Elimelech move to because of the famine?
☐ Bethlehem, Judah   ☒ Moab   ☐ Egypt

Where did they come from?
☒ Bethlehem, Judah   ☐ Moab   ☐ Egypt

Where was Ruth from?
☐ Bethlehem, Judah   ☒ Moab   ☐ Egypt

Moab was a polytheistic nation; Moabites believed in and served many gods. When Naomi and Elimelech moved there because of the famine in Judah, it was a significant move from not only their home but also their cultural and religious customs. It had to be all the more excruciating when Naomi lost her husband and sons in a land that wasn't her home. But the tables were soon turned when Ruth and Orpah were faced with the decision to leave their home of Moab (their culture, religion, and comforts) to follow Naomi back to Judah. Speaking of home, did you notice how many times the word was used? Before my reading yesterday, I never noticed how many times the word home was mentioned. Home was a huge emphasis in the story.

Keeping this in mind, what does Orpah eventually decide in verse 14? *To go back to her parents*

Who and what does Naomi tell Ruth to return to in verse 15? *To her people & her gods.*

The concept of home is a huge deal to me. A few weeks ago Carrie and her husband, John, sold their home—the place where we nogs have had several dinners and deep conversations. They never even called me for approval, which is good cause I wouldn't have signed off. I hate change.

In all seriousness, a sense of home and community is everything to me. This year I had two job offers that would have taken me several states away. Though willing to go at God's leading, I could barely breathe at the thought of leaving my friends and home in Nashville. Though I was thankful and relieved that God didn't end up calling me to physically move, He has been moving me on some heart levels. Physical proximity isn't the only moving God does.

Let me explain … I spoke to a group of young women on this topic last week. A few of the girls expressed a TV addiction that has been hard to break. They said that watching TV gave them a sense of comfort and community. In a sense, it represented home to them. I've privately met with others who expressed that shopping, excessive dependence on a person, food, drinking, or sexual activity had become things they deemed necessary in their lives. They didn't use this word, but all of it was part of their sense of *home*, their sense of security. When it comes to our functional gods, God calls us to move away from them— sometimes it's a physical move, but more often, it's a heart move. One that can be every bit as gut wrenching, but one that promises the presence and satisfaction of God.

Write, word for word, Ruth's response to Naomi in verse 16.

Entreat me not to leave you or turn back from following after you. For where you go, I will go, and wherever you lodge, I will lodge. Your people shall be my people, and your God, my God.

Describe the elements of difficulty for Ruth to leave her people, gods, and sense of security behind.

She wanted to go with Naomi

Two nights ago the nogs gathered at my house. Somehow we got to discussing old boyfriends and youthful romances. Carrie shared this story that was similar to the opening story at the top of this week …

I was going through some old files and came across a bunch of old letters, photos, and other random stuff. I happened to find a few letters from old boyfriends that I thought I had gotten rid of. I knew they didn't have a place in my house anymore. It wasn't about wanting to be back in that situation, or anything, it was just about knowing that my commitment was with my husband that I loved, and there wasn't really room for anything else or the opportunity to open up any past doors in my head.

Leaving is hard. The process often requires walking away from the comfortable and familiar to embrace the new. And sometimes the new doesn't present itself immediately, which is where faith comes in. Sometimes, like Carrie, we've embraced the new, but we don't want to leave opportunities for the old to return. I don't think Ruth knew what she was getting into when she left the gods of her youth behind, but she went regardless. And when she got to Judah, she didn't leave an open door through which to turn back. Tomorrow we'll see what I don't think she could have ever dreamed God had in store for her.

Wherever you are in your journey, I hope you're as moved as I am by the last line in chapter 1 (NIV): "So Naomi returned from Moab accompanied by Ruth the Moabitess, her daughter in-law, arriving in Bethlehem as the _beginning of_ _barley harvest_ **."**

How sweet God's timing! My heart clings to this mention.

It reminds me of Isaiah 43:18-19. Read its hopeful words, knowing that whatever you are being called to leave in your heart, the new will soon be springing up. Make room ... *for God.*

DAY 05 MAKING ROOM
THE HARVEST

I'm excited to pick up where we left off yesterday … as the barley harvest was beginning. Ruth had left her gods and land behind, and now she found herself in Judah, the home of Naomi, her mother-in-law. She had no friends, no security, and no familiarity. But a harvest was springing up in ways that would go far beyond barley.

> **Read Ruth 2:1-23. Let the story line absorb you.**
> **What relative of Naomi owned the field in which Ruth worked?**

Boaz

> **Look at verses 3-4 (NIV) and fill in the blanks:**

> "So she went out and began to glean in the fields behind the harvesters. ___She happened come to the field of Boaz___, she found herself working in a field belonging to Boaz, who was from the clan of Elimelech. ___Now behold___ Boaz arrived from Bethlehem and greeted the harvesters, 'The LORD be with you!'"

I find God's providence in the life of Ruth to be pretty amazing—subtle, but amazing. First we see that she arrives in Judah right as the barley harvest is beginning. Then we see her take a job in a field that just so happens to belong to Boaz who happens to be a relative who happens to arrive right as she's gleaning in his field. I believe this is not coincidence but God's guiding hand moving at just the right time.

> **PERSONAL REFLECTION: Describe a time when you experienced the clear moving of God's hand (it could be a time when others saw it as coincidence, but you knew it to be Providence).**

A dear friend recently came to visit. We have very different worldviews, mine coming from a biblical perspective and his coming from a more humanistic angle. I'm not sure if he believes in God, but he definitely believes in the power of self. As we were talking about the last year, he was very complimentary of my life and the strides I have made. I genuinely responded at how good God has been to me, and how

Ruth 2:12
May you be richly rewarded by the LORD, the God of Israel, under whose wings you have come to take refuge.

He has specifically blessed me in some areas in the past several months. He replied, "Kelly, *you've* done this. *You've* worked hard to attain what you have. Don't sell yourself short. At least meet God halfway."

I mulled this over throughout the week. I know that there is no "meeting God halfway." I know the blessings He has given me are just that—Him giving them. Yes, I have made room in some areas that included some hard choices and hard work, but it was God who brought the increase and filled those spaces. He has asked me to be obedient so He can do the supernatural. I thank Him that He has not met me halfway, because we never would have met. I couldn't have made it that far. Instead, He came all the way to me through Christ and then gave me the grace to follow Him.

> I thank Him that He has not met me halfway, because we never would have met.

We see this concept played out in the life of Ruth. She had made some profoundly difficult choices, and had persevered in some amazing ways, but ultimately it was God who did the supernatural works. He was the One moving the pieces.

Next to each verse, write the ways Ruth showed her perseverance and commitment to hard work.

2:2 *Please let me go to the field & glean heads of grain*

2:3 *She gleaned & happened to glean in Boaz fields*

2:7 *Please let me glean & gather after the reapers*

2:11 *Boaz notices how Ruth left everything.*

2:17-18 *She brought to Naomi what she had gleaned.*

I'm wondering if you happen to be in a "gleaning" season of life—picking up the leftovers to survive. I wonder if you're taking care of a Naomi, in a place where you have few or no friends, or in unfamiliar surroundings (literally or otherwise). I wonder if you're tired and wanting to give up; if you've written things in your journal like *I can't do this anymore* (a common entry for me at one time). I wonder if you're regretting your decision to move from some comfortable idols to make room—perhaps the room feels empty and you're wondering where in the world God is.

If you're in any of these places, I believe you're in the company of Ruth. Remember, the barley harvest was beginning. Still much work remained to be done, but how God was blowing the Spirit winds of change, bringing about an unfathomable harvest for Ruth.

In the meantime, where did Ruth find her refuge (v. 12)? After answering that, write out the whole verse word for word.

Boaz

The Lord repay your works, and a full reward be given you by the Lord God of Israel, under whose wings you have come for refuge.

I love the fact that Ruth—before any major, life-changing blessings had occurred—took refuge under the wings of the God of Israel. This blesses me so much, especially as it relates to the theme of our study: leaving our false gods for the One True God and finding refuge in Him.

Though I wish we could spend several days in this book, my hope is that you will come away with yet another picture of what God can do when we leave our idols to make room for Him. Keep reading …

Skip ahead and read 4:9,13-22.

Ruth left her land and gods behind for the God of Israel. She could have made no better move. Today we spent a lot of time looking at the hard work and probable loneliness Ruth endured in Judah when she first arrived. We looked at her persevering obedience. We saw that she took refuge in the God of Israel under whose wings she had come to trust. We saw the love and loyalty she showed to Naomi. And now we see the blessings—a Moabite woman being married to a high-standing man from Bethlehem. We see a child named Obed. We see a blessed mother-in-law cradling the child in her lap. And, again, not just any child. Obed was the grandfather of King David.

Turn ahead and read Matthew 1:5-6. What female name appears in the lineage of Messiah? *Ruth*

It all goes back to the road that Ruth and her sister-in-law Orpah were on in the beginning of the story. They had to make a decision: stay or go. Ruth chose to follow Naomi back to the land of Judah. To leave her own gods behind. To make the God of Israel her God. To work in the fields. To show loyalty to Naomi. To make room. Her story ends with the advent of Jesus Christ, Who actually never ends. Ruth has an eternal story.

If you're gleaning in the fields, if you're being obedient and you're waiting, if you're learning to take refuge in the God of Israel above all else, keep going … He will do the rest.

> **PERSONAL REFLECTION: End with a personal prayer asking God to keep encouraging you in your obedience. Ask Him to do amazing things beyond anything you could ever imagine.**

Keep track of what the nogs are up to on: *http://www.lifeway.com/ livingroomseries*

With every bend, twist, and dip in the road, we proclaim God faithful.

I speak on behalf of the nogs when I say that we've been privileged to share a little life with you. (Remember to find us on the Web so we can continue the journey.) Also, I know I speak on their behalf when I say that God blesses obedience. All five of us have journeyed together through singleness, marriage, deaths, pregnancy, moves, renovations, job changes, disappointments, and celebratory moments. With every bend, twist, and dip in the road, we proclaim God faithful. We proclaim Him good. We proclaim Him right. And, mostly, we proclaim Him God. As my friend put it, "God with a capital G."

LAURI'S SECRET RECIPE CHILI
SERVES 6

1 lb. ground beef
1 medium onion, diced
4 16 oz. cans of chili beans
2 14.5 oz. cans of diced tomatoes
¼ c. chili powder
1½ T. cumin
1 T. hot sauce
salt and pepper

Fry beef and onion in pan until cooked through over medium-high heat. Salt and pepper lightly to taste.

In an 8-quart pot (or stock pot), combine chili beans and tomatoes. Bring to a boil over medium-high heat. Turn heat down to medium and add beef and onion into pot. Add spices and stir together.

Let it cook at a simmer at least 10 minutes. Add hot sauce (more to taste) and serve!

Top with cheese, sour cream, Fritos, or any favorite chili topping. I like to serve it with some good, warm cornbread!

No Other Gods is a discussion-based Bible study. This leader guide is just that—a guide. The women in your group will come up with their own questions and want to follow different trains of thought. Digging deeper into your own life and sharing with your group will help you grow and form special bonds with your group. Use these questions as a start. While you won't be able to go over every question each week (you'd be there all night!), you can pick the ones that appeal to your group. Feel free to substitute and, in fact, encourage other questions women in your group want to explore.

You may use *No Other Gods* in a variety of settings, at church or in a home-based study. If you can, share a meal together before the study. This is a great time to fellowship and get to know each other's lives without feeling pressure to talk about a specific topic.

You will probably want to take turns cooking even if you meet at the same place each week; that way the burden will not fall on one person. You could also choose to meet at a different woman's home each week and have the host for the week prepare the meal. If your group feels that you absolutely do not have time to have dinner before your discussion time, still try to have a short time of fellowship with coffee and a small dessert (15-30 minutes). Including dinner, your sessions will probably take about 3 hours (1 to 1½ hours for dinner and 1 to 1½ hours for discussion). Without dinner, set aside 1½ to 2 hours (15-30 minutes for fellowship and 1 to 1½ hours for discussion).

Discussion may either take place at the table as you are finishing the meal and enjoying dessert, or you may move to comfortable seating in another room. Part of the delight of having a home-based study is the ability to sit on the couch with your shoes off. However, let the evening go naturally. Your group will inevitably flow to one place or the other.

You'll want to keep your group between four and eight women. If more women are interested, consider splitting into two groups. Because this study is discussion-based rather than leader-based, it is essential that all women feel comfortable speaking up; smaller groups will help this process. It's not necessary to have a specific leader for *No Other Gods;* however, you might want to appoint one woman to look over the questions in advance each week and make any necessary preparations (some weeks involve doing a little research beforehand).

One element that's been important to the "nogs" has been the use of music as a way of incorporating more sensory involvement in the study. You might also consider lighting a scented candle or incense to accentuate the mood (as long as no one is allergic). Between your dinner, discussion, music, and a lovely scent wafting through the house, all of your senses will be tingled by God. We can experience God more fully when we use all of our senses to worship Him. We've provided suggestions for menus, candle scents, and songs for each week in this leader guide.

Many sessions encourage the use of specific items available on the Web site, *www.lifeway.com/livingroomseries*. Make use of the great music downloads, additional recipes, and discussion boards. The more ideas you pursue during the week, the more you will have to talk about on your meeting night!

Remember, these are just suggestions. Identify those areas where you were touched during the week, and bring those up for discussion in your group. Make whatever you want for dinner—there's no need to stick to the provided recipes (although they are all delicious!). Pray together, cry together, and definitely laugh together as you do whatever it takes for you to make room in your life for God.

*Recipes that are available on the Web site, *www.lifeway. com/livingroomseries,* are marked with an asterisk.

01 PERSONAL PHARAOHS

DISCUSSION GUIDE

01. What do you think of Anadara's declaration that she refused to send Christmas cards (p. 10)? What things are you expected to do that you aren't sure you can do anymore? Why?

02. Discuss the question on the bottom of page 13.

03. Review your responses to the prompt on the top of page 15. Are there any new functional gods you've come across this week?

04. Have someone read aloud 1 Corinthians 10:1-13. Can you think of any biblical character who had the same plight or idol you are dealing with? How can this person's story help you to put aside your idol?

05. Discuss the Your Turn response on page 19.

06. Share the situation you wrote about in response to the Personal Reflection prompt on page 20. Did reading about the Israelites make you feel any better or give you any comfort about your situation?

07. Have someone read aloud Isaiah 44:1-20. What insights into idols did you receive from this passage? Discuss your answers to the last question on page 22.

08. Do you have any skills that you have used to create a false god? (See p. 23.)

09. Share your answers from the bottom of page 23. What skills do have that you can use for God's glory? Help one another think you can use your skills in your church or community.

10. Day 5 emphasizes the importance of the heart. How can we protect our hearts against false idols? What about idols that have already made their homes there?

11. If possible, listen to the song "First in My Heart" together. (You can download it on *http://www.lifeway.com/livingroomseries*.) What will it take to make God first in your heart?

12. Share some of your insights from the last question on page 26.

13. End the session by praying together. Pray that God will make room in the hearts of all your members during this eight-week study.

14. Remind members about the Creative Reflection project at the end of week 1 (p. 27). Next week everyone should bring an example to discuss.

MENU

/ BLACK BEANS AND RICE (P. 29)
/ BUTTERFINGER CAKE (P. 28)
/ ICED TEA

CANDLE SCENT

COTTON OR OTHER "CLEAN" SCENT

PLAYLIST

01 DELIVER ME
by Margaret Becker on *Falling Forward*
www.maggieb.com

02 BLACKBIRD
by Sarah McLachlan on *I Am Sam Soundtrack*
www.sarahmclachlan.com

03 USELESS DESIRES
by Patty Griffin on *Impossible Dream*
www.pattygriffin.com

02 WHY IDOLS?

DISCUSSION GUIDE

01. What has kept you from your study this week? Be reminded of the push in the introduction—"Be intentional about your time with God." Encourage each other to make time five days this week for study.

02. Is there one thing you've always thought might help you gain identity? From this week's study, how have you been convicted that this one thing may not deliver what it promises? From where does true identity come?

03. Have someone read aloud 1 Peter 2:9-12. Discuss the first question on page 38.

04. Have you ever come into contact with someone who dressed or acted strangely in the name of Christ? Do you think that's a valid interpretation of 1 Peter 2:11? Why or why not?

05. Have someone read aloud this excerpt from page 39: "I would love it said of my life: The goodness of Jesus Christ burned so brightly in her that people glorified God; she almost seemed from another world." How would you need to be changed by God for this to be said about you?

06. Discuss the first question on page 41.

07. Do you agree that "if it all looks easy and doable, it doesn't require faith" (p. 41)? If so, how has this played out in your life?

08. What are your thoughts in responses to the quote from Oprah at the beginning of day 3 (p. 43)?

09. Turn to page 45. Share answers to the Personal Reflection question at the end of day 3.

10. What are some ways that we turn God's gifts into gods as the Israelites did in Exodus 12?

11. Do you believe it's true that fear is not an idol but something that protects our gods? Why or why not? Talk about your answers to the first question on page 50.

12. Discuss which verses from page 50 struck you the most. What touched you? How did a verse or verses relate to your idols and/or fears?

13. Share prayer requests, especially those relating to fears in your life. Spend a few minutes in silent prayer, perhaps with background music playing. Have one group member close your time in a spoken prayer.

MENU

/ BECKER'S PASTA (P. 52)
/ CAPRESE SALAD (P. 53)
/ SPUMONI ICE CREAM

CANDLE SCENT

AN EXOTIC SCENT, SUCH AS COCONUT OR PINEAPPLE

PLAYLIST

01 THE BLESSING
by John Waller (with Mark Hall of Casting Crowns) on *The Blessing*
www.johnwallermusic.com

· ·

02 TO TRUST YOU
by Ginny Owens on *Beautiful*
www.ginnyowens.com

· ·

03 SMALL ENOUGH
by Nichole Nordeman on *This Mystery*
www.nicholenordeman.com

03 LIES

DISCUSSION GUIDE

01. In the introduction you read, "I recall the many situations where I wedged myself into something I just knew would bring relief from the scorching heat, but it left me suffocating instead." Do you have any examples of this from your life?

02. Have you become addicted to things that are "pleasing to the eye"? Why is this so dangerous?

03. Discuss your answers to the Personal Reflection question on page 60.

04. Look back at the first few questions on day 2 (p. 61). Were all three things the serpent said about the fruit true? If you answered yes, why is that a frightening fact?

05. Share responses to the prompt on the bottom of page 62.

06. Discuss your response to the Personal Reflection prompt on page 63.

07. How is redemption "something that [God] is passionate to carry out now" (p. 64)? How do we move from considering our salvation experience as a one-time event to seeing it as a continual redemption?

08 Sometimes we second guess our ability to hear God, wondering, "Did I really hear God right when He said ...?" How do you deal with such questions?

09. Discuss the Personal Reflection question on page 69.

10. Is there anything you've been convicted to give up this week? If so, tell about it.

11. If you are comfortable sharing, discuss some lies you have believed about yourself. What truths in Scripture contradict these lies? Build one another up with Scripture as you close your discussion for this week.

MENU

/ CARRIE'S CHICKEN SCALLOPINI WITH ANGEL-HAIR PASTA (P. 75)
/ CAESAR SALAD
/ GARLIC BREAD
/ EASY PEACH COBBLER*

CANDLE SCENT

ROSE

PLAYLIST

01 LIAR'S DREAM
by Alli Rogers on *Day of Small Things*
www.allirogers.com

....

02 JUST ISAAC
by Margaret Becker on *Air*
www.maggieb.com

....

03 MUCH FARTHER TO GO
by Rosie Thomas on *These Friends of Mine*
www.rosiethomas.com

04 THE PROBLEM WITH IDOLS

DISCUSSION GUIDE

01. Have you ever created scenarios in our head that allowed you to believe lies about yourself, as Anadara did (pp. 77-78)? If so, what lies do you believe because of this inclination?

02. Why do you think God often tells us what to do and then shows us why? Where do you see examples of this in Bible? in your life?

03. Did you answer yes or no to the last question on page 81? Share examples to explain your answer.

04. Review the question and last two paragraphs on page 83. How do you feel about James' use of the word *adulteress* in this passage?

05. Share responses to the writing prompt on the bottom of page 84, if you are comfortable doing so.

06. Respond to the exercise on page 86 involving the names of Leah's children. Have someone read aloud Genesis 29:32-35. What do you think of the meaning of Judah's name? Keep in mind that Jesus is from the line of Judah. Based on what you know of the rest of the story, do you think Leah was truly healed and rid of her idol when she had Judah?

07. As you are willing, discuss your response to the Personal Reflection prompt on page 87.

08. Turn to page 89. Share your responses to either or both of the Personal Reflection prompts.

09. On page 93 you read, "People will do far crazier things when something threatens their ultimate thing." Can you think of examples from the Bible or from current news?

10. In day 5 each person was asked to complete three readings of Colossians 3:1-17. If most members have done this, discuss what you found insightful from each reading. If it seems that many members skipped the exercise, do it together now. Read from three different translations if possible. Discuss what stands out to you from each reading and what new insights God has given you.

MENU

/ ALLI'S THAI ICED TEA*
/ PUMPKIN MUFFINS (P. 97)
/ EASY BEEF POT ROAST (P. 96)

CANDLE SCENT

A LIGHT SCENT, SUCH AS STRAWBERRY OR MELON

PLAYLIST

01 BEAUTY
by Ayiesha Woods on
Introducing Ayiesha Woods
www.ayieshawoods.com

02 BROKEN PLACES
by Ashley Cleveland on *Second Skin*
www.ashleycleveland.com

03 WORLDS APART
by Jars of Clay on *Jars of Clay*
www.jarsofclay.com

04 THE KINGDOM
by Bethany Dillon on *Waking Up*
www.bethanydillon.com

05 GOOD GOODBYES

DISCUSSION GUIDE

01. Turn to the question at the bottom of page 103. Without getting into specific idols, unless you feel that pull, discuss how craving an idol is different than wanting or needing it.

02. Discuss the Your Take question on page 105.

03. What does it mean to say God "over-fills" our desire for sin (see p. 105)? Is God just being spiteful? What are some good reasons that He might "over-fill" our lusts? Have there been times when this has happened to you? If so, share as you are willing.

04. Before the session, use a Web site such as *www.biblegateway. com* to find all the instances of the word fruit in the Bible. Have someone paste some of these Scriptures into a document and make a copy for each member (or e-mail it to everyone ahead of time). What role does fruit play in the Bible? What will God do if we stop bearing fruit or bear bad fruit? Why is it so important to bear fruit? How is Christ the "branch" to believers? (See Lev. 27:30; Num. 13:20; Deut. 29:18; Prov. 12:12; Is. 3:10; 11:1; Hos. 10:13; Matt. 7:16-20; 21:43; John 15:1-16; Rom. 6:22; Gal. 5:22; Jas. 5:7; Rev. 22:2.)

05. Discuss the Personal Reflection question on page 108.

06. Do you agree that God's promises are not necessarily realized without struggle? Why or why not? What obstacles are you currently experiencing in your pursuit of a promise God has given you? Take turns sharing promises from Scripture you have claimed as well as some you have has trouble claiming.

07. Revisit the story of Jesus and the rich young ruler (Mark 10:17-31). Read it aloud in your group, if you desire. How does Christ show us His love by telling us our faults and pointing out the things we need to get rid of?

08. How does Jesus come and help you "clean up your mess"? Why do we try to keep it from Him when He already knows it's there? Do you tend to think of God more like a mother telling you to clean your room or else, or like a dear friend who will help you out? Why?

09. Reflecting on day 5, have you ever considered Isaac to be an idol of his father, Abraham? Do you think that perhaps Sarah wasn't the only one obsessed with having a child? Why or why not? Abraham went immediately ("early the next morning," Gen. 22:3) to sacrifice his son after God told him to. What does this tell you about Abraham's attachment to this idol?

10. Put on a worship CD. Pray together the prayer of A.W. Tozer found at the end of day 5 (p. 118). Afterward, have a "popcorn" prayer, allowing group members to pray for specific needs in their own lives and idols they need help letting go of.

MENU

/ SICILIAN PIZZA CRUST WITH YOUR FAVORITE TOPPINGS (P. 119)
/ STRAWBERRY SALAD WITH BALSAMIC VINAIGRETTE*
/ ALLI'S OATMEAL CHOCOLATE CHIP COOKIES*

CANDLE SCENT

GRAPEFRUIT OR OTHER CITRUS

PLAYLIST

01 SONG OF MY SURRENDER
by Anadara on *Into the Unknown*
www.anadara.com

02 I WILL BE FREE
by Cindy Morgan on *A Reason to Live*
www.cindymorganmusic.com

03 THERE IS A RIVER
by Jars of Clay on *Good Monsters*
www.jarsofclay.com

04 THE STORY
by Brandi Carlile on *The Story*
www.brandicarlile.com

06 GOD OF GODS

DISCUSSION GUIDE

01. What "spiritual guitar cases" have you never opened? Which ones have you opened but refused to "play"?

02. Discuss your response to the Personal Reflection prompt on page 127.

03. Have someone read the following excerpt from page 130 aloud: "Our soul does not delight in God over a Scripture-memory verse or church attendance or doing a Bible study alone. It delights in Him when we come, listen, turn from our idols, and call out to Him." How have you used this study as a tool to do those things?

04. What practical steps can we take toward improving our ability to sit, listen, and call on God?

05. What images come to mind when you hear the phrase "delight in the richest of fare"? How does this make you see differently what God has set before you?

06. Which psalm did you pick from page 131 to meditate on? What did you glean from your careful reading of it?

07. How does it make you feel to know that the Holy Spirit "yearns jealously" for your attention (Jas. 4:5, HCSB)?

08. Take turns sharing your comparisons of your prominent functional god and the God of gods (p. 136).

09. Have you ever had an experience with a physical idol, similar to Alli's experience with the Athena statue? If so, share it with the group.

10. Have one person in your group read aloud all of Isaiah 46. What images jump out at you from this Scripture? How does it make you feel about your idols?

11. Recall some of the bullet points you wrote on page 139 related to how God has sustained and blessed you. Share these blessings with your group. How has He "upheld [you] since you were conceived, and … carried you since your birth"? (See Isa. 46:3.)

12. At the end of day 5, how did the act of bowing down before God change you? What attributes of God have shown themselves to you this week?

13. If you feel so led, have everyone in the group get on her knees before God. Pray together, honoring God with your bodies.

MENU

/ GRANDMA'S MAC AND CHEESE (P. 140)
/ PAULA'S TOSSED SALAD (P. 141)
/ WARM CHOCOLATE CAKE WITH ICE CREAM

CANDLE SCENT

VANILLA

PLAYLIST

01 OH HOW YOU LOVE ME
by Rita Springer on *All I Have*
www.ritaspringer.com

02 REDEEMER
by Nicole C. Mullen on *Nicole C. Mullen*
www.nicolecmullen.com

03 GIVE ME JESUS
by Fernando Ortega on *Hymns of Worship*
www.fernandoortega.com

04 EVERLASTING GOD
by Brenton Brown on *Everlasting God*
www.brentonbrownmusic.com

07 THE ROAD AHEAD

DISCUSSION GUIDE

01. Consider this quote from the introduction: "There are things that we can't make sense of. Things that sometimes our idols can explain much better. And when they can't explain them, they can at least make us feel really good in our confusion" (p. 145). What examples of this have you seen in your life?

02. Turn to page 148 and discuss your answers to the second question (beginning, "Can you think of a time…").

03. What definition of legalism did you give on page 150? How did you tie Matthew 23:25-26 into your definition?

04. How does Romans 10:3 pertain to legalism?

05. Discuss your answers to the last question on page 150. Have someone read aloud 2 Chronicles 6:34-40. What in this passage stands out to you? What reassures you?

06. Skim through the last paragraph on page 150. Can anyone relate to this experience?

07. What area of your life did you describe in response to the third question on page 149 (beginning, "Write about …")?

08. Read the following aloud: "No matter how disciplined a person may be, she will have weaknesses in her life. Sometimes the discipline itself is to compensate for or cover up a weakness" (p. 153). Have you had this experience or seen it in others?

09. One of the biblical focuses of day 3 is Paul's thorn in the flesh. Discuss the following questions: Why do you think Paul didn't tell us what his thorn in the flesh was? What does the fact that Paul's thorn was not removed despite his pleading with God tell you about prayer? about God? What do you think a "messenger of Satan" is?

10. Have someone read aloud Genesis 50:20 Share responses to the third question on page 154 (beginning, "Can you think of a time …").

11. Do you agree that surrender is about the will and trust is about the heart? Why or why not?

12. What did you think of chapter 2 of the Book of Jonah? Skim through it quickly. Is Jonah thanking God that he was swallowed by a whale? Why is he praising God? Why do you think he goes from praising God in chapter 2 to cursing God (ch. 4) so rapidly?

13. Discuss the last question of day 4 (p. 158). If you feel led, have one member read Psalm 121 aloud while others listen with eyes closed.

14. Share about your experience of praying Scripture at the end of day 5. Were you given any new revelations? What Scriptures jumped out at you?

MENU

/ CHICKEN CUTLETS (P. 160)
/ MOM'S SAUCE (P. 161)
/ FRESH GREEN BEANS
/ ITALIAN BREAD WITH BUTTER
/ ITALIAN SODAS*

CANDLE SCENT

LAVENDER

PLAYLIST

01 DARE YOU TO MOVE
by Switchfoot on *The Beautiful Letdown*
www.switchfoot.com

······································

02 BRING IT ALL TOGETHER
by Natalie Grant (with Wynonna) on *Awaken*
www.nataliegrant.com

······································

03 CRAWL
by Margaret Becker on *Falling Forward*
www.maggieb.com

······································

04 WHEN IT DOESN'T COME EASY
by Patty Griffin on *Impossible Dream*
www.pattygriffin.com

08 MAKING ROOM

DISCUSSION GUIDE

01. Did you relate to the story in the week's introduction (pp. 162-65)? Do you have something physical that represents an emotional attachment or idol that needs to go?

02. Discuss your answers to the first question on page 169.

03. Do you ever have an overwhelming need to explain your decisions? When do you find it difficult to rest quietly in your convictions with the Lord? When is this the wise choice? When should you fight to explain our decisions or convictions?

04. Discuss the Personal Reflection question on page 169.

05. Share responses to the prompt on page 172.

06. A pastor once said that God takes a risk by blessing individuals with intelligence, creativity, and gifts. How is that true? How does it relate to Deuteronomy 8:17-18, which we read in day 3?

07. Discuss your answers to the Personal Reflection questions on page 175.

08. What did you find interesting in the Book of Ruth? What connections did you make to the rest of this study? Have someone read aloud Ruth 1:16-17. What strikes you most in Ruth's response to Naomi? Could you make this kind of sacrifice and stay with someone who was not a blood relative?

09. Share responses to the Personal Reflection prompt on page 179.

10. Do you feel like you're in a gleaning period of life? Read aloud the last full paragraph on page 180. Are any of these feelings familiar—perhaps a little too familiar? How do you relate to Ruth and her struggles?

11. Ruth and Boaz's first son was named Obed, which means "servant." Why is this fitting?

12. One decision in Ruth's life—to stay with her mother-in-law—had incredible consequences. Because of this decision, she became part of the lineage of Jesus. Have you ever made a decision you thought was small at the time that turned into something huge for you? What decisions are you facing that might have great consequences—negative or positive—down the road?

13. This is your final week together, so you will want to celebrate in a special way! Perhaps you would like to go around the group and take turns sharing something poignant that has happened to you during this study. Perhaps you would like to spend time in prayer for one another after sharing requests (silent or aloud). Maybe sharing Scriptures that have been meaningful to you would be helpful. Decide as a group. Close in a prayer of thanksgiving to the God for Whom we are making room.

MENU

/ LAURI'S SECRET RECIPE CHILI (P. 183)
/ SWEET CORNBREAD
/ CREME CARAMEL*

CANDLE SCENT

SUGAR COOKIE, CAKE BATTER, OR OTHER "HOMEY" SCENT

PLAYLIST

01 FIRST
by Carl Cartee on *First*
www.carlcartee.com

02 TO KNOW YOU
by Nichole Nordeman on *Wide Eyed*
www.nicholenordeman.com

03 NOTHING WITHOUT YOU
by Bebo Norman on *Try*
www.bebonorman.com

04 ALL I NEED
by Margaret Becker on *Air*
www.maggieb.com